Real

Transurfing

VOLUME II
THE RUSTLING OF THE
MORNING STARS

First published by O Books, 2008
O Books is an imprint of John Hunt Publishing
Ltd., The Bothy, Deershot Lodge, Park Lane,
Ropley, Hants, SO24 0BE, UK
office1@o-books.net
www.o-books.net

Distribution in:

UK and Europe
Orca Book Services
orders@orcabookservices.co.uk
Tel: 01202 665432 Fax: 01202 666219 Int. code
(44)

USA and Canada
NBN
custserv@nbnbooks.com
Tel: 1 800 462 6420 Fax: 1 800 338 4550

Australia and New Zealand
Brumby Books
sales@brumbybooks.com.au
Tel: 61 3 9761 5535 Fax: 61 3 9761 7095

Far East (offices in Singapore, Thailand, Hong
Kong, Taiwan)
Pansing Distribution Pte Ltd
kemal@pansing.com
Tel: 65 6319 9939 Fax: 65 6462 5761

South Africa
Alternative Books
altbook@peterhyde.co.za
Tel: 021 555 4027 Fax: 021 447 1430

Text copyright Vadim Zeland 2008

Design: Stuart Davies

ISBN: 978 1 84694 131 3

A CIP catalogue record for this book is available
from the British Library.

This first volume translated by Natasha Micharina
First published in Russian under the title
Трансерфинг реальности Ступень I:
Пространство вариантов by Ves Publishing,
197101, 6 Mira St. Petersburg, Russia

Printed by Digital Book Print

O Books operates a distinctive and ethical publishing philosophy in
all areas of its business, from its global network of authors to
production and worldwide distribution.

Reality Transurfing

VOLUME II
THE RUSTLING OF THE
MORNING STARS

Vadim Zeland

Translated by Natasha Micharina

Books in the series

Reality Transurfing 1:
The Space of Variations

Reality Transurfing 2:
A Rustle of Morning Stars

Reality Transurfing 3:
Forward to the Past

BOOKS

Winchester, UK
Washington, USA

CONTENTS

Chapter I. Intention   1

Where do dreams come from? Are they simply a product of human imagination? What do dreams and reality have in common? The curtain is being lifted, unveiling the secrets of ancient magicians who built the Egyptian pyramids and other similar structures.

Chapter II. Slides   53

Why are desires not fulfilled, and dreams do not come true? In order to make the things you want your reality, you need to know how to make an "order". Starting with this chapter and onwards, you will be provided with specific practical recommendations on how to manifest your order in reality. These are the first steps of a magician.

Chapter III. Your Soul and Your Mind

Man possesses great power, which is sometimes referred to as psychic energy. Everyone has magic abilities, but they are deeply buried within. Apparently, you do not have to go to great lengths to unlock your inner reserves and potential. The wondrous is just around the corner, but humans don't notice it.

Chapter IV. Goals and Doors

Each person has their own path where they will gain true happiness. But how do you find this path? You are about to find out. And since your desires do not always match your possibilities, how do you reach the goal you have set before you? You shall see for yourself that your possibilities are only limited by your intention. By breaking the locks of stereotypes, you are opening the doors that previously seemed inaccessible.

Note on Translation

In this volume, the soul is referred to in its feminine form and the mind in its masculine form, both according to the original gender form in the Russian language. As both soul and mind are two very important concepts in the book it is necessary to convey the author's attempt to attribute almost human-like characteristics to these two concepts. Important imagery and nuances in the tone of the book would have otherwise been lost

Also in accordance with the convention of the language the book has been translated in its original masculine form (He, Man, Mankind etc.)

FOREWORD

All of us are one way or another, in the power of circumstances. Desires are unfulfilled, dreams do not come true, yet our worst fears, as ill luck would have it, are realized. Can't it really be the other way around? Turns out – it can. And you shall find out how that is possible.

This book will open a very strange world before you, where every day reality appears in an unfamiliar form. Many vitally important questions are examined from a completely unexpected point of view. But it is not the unusualness of this new reality that is the most striking, but rather the fact that you can control this reality.

Transurfing – is a technique of controlling reality, and it is a rather peculiar one too. In Transurfing, the goal is not being reached; it is instead being realized mostly on its own. This sounds incredible only in the framework of the ordinary worldview. We shall have to tear down the wall of settled stereotypes and false limitations.

Indeed, submitting reality to your will is a rather difficult thing to do. Sacred wishes and bold dreams are truly hard to achieve, if you are to follow the generally accepted norms and rules. It is well known how futile and sometimes idle the attempts to change yourself or the world around you can be.

Transurfing offers a fundamentally different way of thinking and acting so that you get what you want. Not to push, but to actually get what you want. Not to change yourself, but to return to yourself.

The main idea of Transurfing is based on the assumption that there is such a thing as the space of variations, where all possible scripts of all possible events are stored. The number of variations is infinite, just as the multiplicity of possible locations of a point on a coordinate grid. Everything that was, is and will be is recorded in the space of variations. The energy of a person's thoughts is, under certain circumstances, able to materialize a particular sector in the space of variations.

Potential possibility is materialized into reality, like a reflection in the mirror of variations. Men and women are able to shape their reality. But in order to do that, one has to follow certain rules. The human mind is trying to affect the reflection without any luck, while it is the actual image itself that has to be changed.

What is this image? How do you change it? How do you handle this strange mirror? Transurfing provides the answers to all of these questions. And only one thing remains unsolved: what hides there, behind the mirror?

Despite the fantastic nature of the ideas that are presented in this book, they have already been practically confirmed. Those, who tried to practice Transurfing, experienced astonishment bordering on ecstasy. The surrounding world of the transurfer is, in some incredible way, changing right before his eyes. Now it is no longer virtual mysticism, but a controllable reality instead.

CHAPTER I

INTENTION

Where do dreams come from? Are they simply a product of human imagination? What do dreams and reality have in common? The curtain is being lifted, unveiling the secrets of ancient magicians who built the Egyptian pyramids and other similar structures. Your possibilities are limited only by your intention.

Waking Up in Your Dream

In this chapter, we are getting even closer to solving the Riddle of the Overseer: why we are able to choose anything we want, and how we should go about doing it. One of the clues to this riddle lies within a phenomenon we call dreaming. A person spends one third of his life sleeping and dreaming. Everything that happens to him in this borderland has, up until now, been under a veil of secrecy. Unfortunately, scientific research in this area offers little explanation. Philosophical interpretations are also moving from one extreme to another. Some say that dreams are simply illusions; others claim that our life itself is nothing but a dream. Who is right? Within the framework of the Transurfing model – no one is right. But let's not rush ahead.

When remembering their dreams, adults are aware of the fact that nothing actually happened to them. Their minds interpret dreams as fantasies that somehow take place when people rest. The human mind is satisfied with such an explanation. It is well known that children up to four years of age do not differentiate between dream and reality, where they are awake. They believe that dreams take place in the same world as the rest of their life. At that age, having woken up from a nightmare, completely terrified, a child would think that monsters are still in the room. And any attempts on the part of the parents to reassure their child that it was all just a dream, fail to have the desired effect. Nevertheless, the child's mind will gradually be trained and will get accustomed to the thought that dreams are not real.

We have already discussed how our mind organizes any new incoming information by abstract labeling. And he does so willingly and extremely fast. But imagine this: it took four years to convince our mind that dreams are unreal. This is the only idea the mind had difficulties in accepting. We do not remember anything before the age of four. Therefore, we could not have witnessed the bewilderment experienced by our mind upon awakening from his dream.

But even now, every day when our mind gets disconnected, it keeps falling simple-heartedly into the same trap. While we are asleep, it wouldn't occur to us to critically examine the ongoing events. And even upon waking up, we are amazed at how real the dream seemed to be. A dream's virtual reality is modeled in a strikingly natural way. In spite of the fact that the oddest things happen in our dreams most of the time, we perceive them as something ordinary. This ability is based on the mind's tendency to find explanations for everything. If we are to notice or experience anything extraordinary, we are always ready to rationalize it. Then again, we are not used to questioning the reality of events when we are awake and conscious. Hence, even in our dreams we automatically interpret everything as a matter of course. Our mind is used to controlling situations. But there is one question, which always passes that control without further inspection: "Is this actually happening?" This is precisely why our mind keeps falling into the dreaming trap.

But sometimes, if we are lucky, a miracle takes place, and we realize that we are sleeping, while asleep. This happens mostly when we dream of something particularly incredible or when a nightmare becomes overly annoying. Consequently, the mind resumes its control, and we are pondering what to do next. In this case, unconscious dreaming becomes conscious, *lucid dreaming*. In a lucid dream the dreamer takes part in the virtual game, but at the same time he is aware of the fact that it's all nothing but a dream. If you have never experienced this phenomenon and it is the first time you hear about it, have no doubts – it is not a flight of imagination.

But don't you want to try? Yes, it is possible to have a lucid dream on purpose. Although, in order to do that you would need to teach your mind to ask the following question: "Is this actually happening?" It is not a hard thing to do, if you truly want to experience a lucid dream. The procedure of teaching your mind is simple, but it does require goal directed attention. You would need to ask yourself the above mentioned question at least ten times a day. Your inner Watcher will help you in this task. Order him to constantly bother you with the question: are you sleeping or not? You should answer this question with maximum awareness, so that there is genuine control taking place, and not just a routine procedure. Rouse yourself, look around and evaluate the situation: is everything as it should be or is something suspicious going on? With enough determination, you will soon wake up in your own dream.

As you will find out, asking yourself a question at least ten times a day is rather difficult. You will simply forget about it. Significant results require a strong desire for a lucid dream to occur. Depending on the power of your intention, the lucid dream will come to you in a few days or perhaps in a few months.

A striking clock (if you have one at home) can be useful in this situation. During the day, every day when the clock strikes, you may turn to your Watcher. He can then ask you whether you are sleeping or not. The sound of the clock will turn into an anchor, a hook that will catch on to your consciousness. And if you hear the striking of the clock in your dream, you will poke your Watcher by habit, and he will in turn awaken your mind. You may find other "hooks" that will be audible even when you are sleeping. Just don't tie the question to signals that cannot be heard in your sleep. For example, if you tie your question to the ring signal of your phone, then you won't be able to ask yourself the question in your sleep until you dream of a phone ringing.

Basically, the idea is to create a habit of constantly asking yourself whether what is happening around you is real or not. Don't answer the question automatically, do it consciously. To many dreamers, recognizing anomalous phenomena, inconsistencies and odd things in their dream is the defining factor in awakening consciousness. In most cases, such things go unnoticed and are perceived as quite normal. That is exactly why you should teach yourself to critically assess each situation and answer the question conscientiously.

Why should you do this? First of all, and at the very least, it is interesting and amusing when your dream is not just simply "happening" to you but when you are playing an active and a conscious part in this virtual game. This is, however, not just some science fiction about virtual reality. No computer game can match what you are able to do in a lucid dream. And you can do anything you want.

When an unwanted situation occurs in your dream, you can easily change it by applying a little willpower. For example, you are having a nightmare: someone is following you, and you cannot shake him off. If you believe that what is happening to you in your dream is real, getting rid of the stalker will be a problem. But if you would realize that you are only dreaming, it is most likely that you would try to wake up, and although with some difficulty, you would succeed most of the time. However, there is a more efficient and more interesting way of getting rid of an unpleasant dream. If you have realized that what you are experiencing is simply a dream, it will be enough to look at the stalker and think: "Go away!" (Vanish, be gone.) The stalker will immediately disappear. You can even get him in the air and make him do somersaults by simply thinking about it.

In his dream, a person is able to fully control everything that is going on by fulfilling two simple conditions. Firstly, he has to realize that it is just a dream. Secondly, he has to know that "here" he can do anything he wants. For example, you have woken up in your dream and want to do some flying. This is extremely easy, because you only need an intention to do it. Here, the difference between desire and intention becomes quite apparent. Simply wishing to get up in the air will get you nowhere, and it doesn't matter if you are awake or dreaming. Let's take, for example, the desire to lift your arm. You are telling yourself that you want to lift your arm. However, you are not doing it just yet. And then, you simply lift your arm. Your wish has been transformed into action. You are not thinking about how you will be lifting your arm, you are simply doing it. It works the same in your dreams: simply get yourself in the air by using pure intention, and fly wherever you want.

Now, let's get back to the nightmare with a stalker. You have to understand by now that wishing for him to disappear would not get you anywhere. When you are ridden with fear, your thoughts are quickly going through all possible alternatives of how the events may develop, and these thoughts of yours are instantly made real. You are involved in a game where the rules are dictated by someone or something else but you. And even if you have realized that it is all just a dream, you won't be able to do anything, unless you take control of things. As long as you are playing the part of a passive victim, you are trapped in the game. It doesn't matter that the game was created by your own imagination. At this point, you are being a slave to your imagination, you are afraid and you run away, because you chose to play that part. Yet, if you stop and decide that you want to swap roles with your stalker, he will happily agree to it and start running away from you. Can you imagine how funny that will look?

The answer to *any* question that begins with "In my dream, can I...?" will be affirmative. You can socialize with anyone (living or dead), do anything you want with items and other actors that appear in your dream, you can fly to other planets, solve problems, make music, rehearse, travel and so on. Heavy drugs, in comparison to all of this, are pure child's play. Besides, there is no health risk involved. You can bring any information with you from your dream. Only one thing is impossible though: bringing a material object from your dream into reality. Anyway, I personally do not know anything about such phenomena.

If you cannot remember what you were dreaming of, try to establish the direction in which you are lying as you sleep. The best alternative is to sleep with your head towards the North. Do not sleep towards the West, as it is not good for your health. I cannot really explain why that is. But it has something to do with the Earth's magnetic field. Try to sleep with your head towards the North, and you will soon discover that your dreams have become more interesting and more colorful.

If lucid dreams won't come to you or you have no wish to pursue this matter, do not worry. Lucid dreaming plays a particular part in the Transurfing practice, but you can do well without it. In addition, there is a concealed threat in lucid dreaming. Oh great, you'll say, first you make us interested and then you threaten us. However, I have no choice. Lucid dreaming is a secret door to the unknown. It would be irresponsible of me not to warn you about the danger that might be lurking behind that door. You shall soon find out what this danger really is.

The Space of Dreams
In order to explain The Riddle of the Overseer, we would need to answer two questions: why is anything possible in lucid dreams? And why do dreams appear to be so real?

In a lucid, as well as in an unconscious dream, you are able to see images very clearly, down to the smallest detail. Sometimes dreams may even exceed reality in their vividness of color and sharpness of form. There is a hypothesis that our brain is gener- ating these images, and when we are asleep, our brain perceives the images in our dream to be as if we were awake. This is actually nothing more than a hypothesis. As of yet, no one has been able to prove that this is how things really happen. The model of Transurfing interprets the phenomenon of dreaming in a very different way: *the subconscious is not imagining anything on its own. Instead, it is connected directly to the space of variations, which contains all of the information.*

Take a close look at a random object, and then close your eyes and try to imagine that very same object. Even if you possess outstanding visualization skills, you will not be able to "see" the object with your eyes closed just as you would, if you had your eyes open. The visual representation of the object that was made by your brain is nothing more than a very low quality photograph. Let us assume that the brain stores this photograph as a particular configuration of neuronal activity. Despite the huge number of neurons in our brain, there will never be enough neurons to recall all of the photographic memories stored in our brain.

If our memories and dreams are only a reproduction of what is "written" in neurons, then how many of these cells are there in our head? Within the framework of Transurfing, neurons are not considered information carriers like bytes in a computer. *The brain does not contain actual information, but something that resembles addresses to the information in the space of variations.*

Possibly, our brain is able to store a limited amount of data. However, despite the fact that our brain is a perfect biological system, it is unable to store everything we are ready to recall from our memory. Even more so, our brain is unable to generate such a complete virtual reality as a dream. Is it easy to close your eyes and picture the made up images in your mind just as naturally as you would if you were dreaming? Don't be deluding yourself with weak arguments that once the brain is "off", it gains the ability to perceive the images it creates more clearly.

As mentioned, our mind is unable to create anything fundamentally new. It is only able to reassemble old bricks into a new version of a house. Our mind has primitive knowledge of these bricks and about how to assemble them. He keeps any further details on paper or other information carriers. Any other information comes to mind through the soul, from the space of variations.

In such way, the mind in the model of Transurfing appears to be a rather primitive system, the activity of which can be technically simulated, and that is what the scientists of today are trying to do. The attempts to create artificial intelligence have yet been unsuccessful. The mind is somehow able to understand itself, but it is yet unable to understand the nature of the soul. The secret behind the intellect of a living being is the unity and interaction between the mind and the soul of that living being. Until now, the efforts of scientists conducting research in cybernetics have been aimed at creating a model of the cognitive processes that take place in a real human mind. But maybe one day, someone will think of making a machine that will be able to tune into the space of variations and obtain information from it, just as our soul does.

Somehow, our mind is able to remember the addresses to the right sectors of space. If you need to remember something, your mind turns to your soul, and the soul in turn tunes into the corresponding sector. Yet, either our soul doesn't do a very good job tuning in, or our mind is bad at remembering addresses, or the soul and the mind cannot come to an agreement about things – either way, the bottom line is that we have what we have: our memory is not perfect.

Nonetheless, our soul is able to randomly tune into the sectors in the space of variations that have yet not been realized, and these are the images we see in our dreams. That is exactly the reason to why this bordering space is so real. *Dreams are not illusions in the ordinary sense of this word. The mind is not imagining dreams, but it is actually seeing them.*

It is a known fact that in a dream, a person may perceive images as if they were out of this world. For example, one could see every detail of an architectural construction, and it is completely obvious that this person could actually never have encountered anything like that. If a dream is only an imitation of reality made by our brain, then where do these never before seen images come from?

As you recall, sectors in the space of variations contain different variations of scripts and decorations. Decorations consist of both inanimate surroundings and living beings. If you have seen your relatives or friends in one of your dreams, you must have noticed that they were not just the way they were or are in real life. They may have a different hairstyle, strange clothes and they may even have a different personality. Virtual characters from the space of dreams may behave a bit unusual and odd. You recognize your friends in your dream, you understand that these are your friends, but at the same time, you feel that there is something not quite right about them. This is how the multiformity of the space of variations appears. Decorations of various sectors differ from one another. Events that we see in reality are realized variations. In our dreams, we get to see a few sectors that have not (yet) been realized.

If, while dreaming, you ever have the chance to see your own reflection in the mirror, you will probably be unpleasantly surprised or frightened. The face in the mirror wouldn't be the same face that you are used to seeing in a real mirror. You will immediately realize that you are you, but your face has changed! The thing is that the way a person looks corresponds to the sector that person happens to be in. Depending on how far away the viewed virtual sector is from the current sector (that has been realized and that is now your reality), your physical appearance will change to a greater or lesser degree.

The surroundings will also change depending on how far the virtual sector is from the realized one. You see your town, but it does not look right. The same streets and houses appear somewhat peculiar to you. You are puzzled, as if you have been hallucinating. If in your dream, you soul has gone far enough from her real sector, then you might find yourself in a completely unfamiliar environment. You will see landscapes and people that do not exist in real life. Everything is living its own virtual life in that sector. And what is then your role in that life? Everything that happens there is immaterial. Your role is just as virtual as the virtual reality you are in. Yet, at the same time, it is not an illusion.

At this point, there can be two options: either the variation of your person exists in that sector or it does not. If your person exists in that sector, would you be able to meet your double? That is a very difficult question, which I am yet unable to answer. It is most likely that your soul takes up the role that is written in the script of the sector. The fact that the dreamer views his face in the mirror as belonging to someone else speaks in favor of the above assumption.

There is one more question that is of interest to us: if information in the space of variations is stored in a static state, like a film reel on a shelf, then why do we see movement in our dreams and take part in this virtual game? All events are stored simultaneously in that field of information. Everything that has been and that is going to happen is already in the field. Then why does the soul, when flying about in the space of variations, see movement of life and not static images? Perhaps our perception works in such a way that we are only able to perceive the movement of a film reel. Or maybe such is the quality of space, and it appears to us only as a flow of variations. If our soul is flying along the sectors, then it does see movement. In that case, where does your soul go when you are dreaming? Where does it travel in time – the past, the present or the future?

Everything concerning the space of dreams carries more questions than answers. I can say one thing for sure: dreams are not an illusion. You got a little scared there, right? Every night, we all travel to the space of variations and there - we live through a virtual life. This virtual life has no tangible physical basis, and nonetheless, it is real.

What could be said about interpreting dreams and the meaning of dreams? The answer might seem a bit surprising to you. You probably assume that in the light of everything mentioned in this book, dreams have the full right to be the harbingers of future events. However, specifically in the light of everything that was previously mentioned, dreams in Transurfing cannot be viewed as the kind of signs we spoke about in the previous chapter.

Dreams show us what *could have been* in the past or in the future. We know the past. The future in the space of variations is too diverse. Therefore, there is no guarantee that we saw an upcoming sector in our dream that is about to be made real. Adjacent sectors actually do have similar scripts and decorations. However, no one can guarantee that the sector you saw in your dream is actually close to your current life track.

In reality, your soul is actually able to sense upcoming events. The most reliable sign is the state of emotional comfort of your soul. When you are awake, your soul displays the state it is in, in relation to the current life track or in relation to the upcoming turn in the flow of variations. Other signs are also related to the *realized* current sector and to its adjacent sectors. Yet, when you are dreaming only God knows the whereabouts of your soul. She could be anywhere, and therefore you cannot rely on the information she brings you.

The next question: if a dream is not a product of our imagination, then who decides what the script of our dreams should be? The script lies in sectors in the space of variations. While the mind is sleeping, the soul may travel in the space of variations anyway it wants to. Sometimes our mind sleeps so heavily that we do not remember our dreams. No one knows what happens to the soul when the mind is sleeping. In real life, the behavior of any person is controlled by the mind. So, when the mind is watching dreams, he plays the role of a passive observer. He does not control the situation but assumes that everything is just the way it should be.

Everything that happens does so according to the script that lies within a particular sector. As soon as your soul steps into that sector, the events of that sector develop in accordance with expectations, fears and ideas acquired by your soul and mind in real life. Expectations and fears are immediately realized. For example, if somebody appears that according to your mind could mean trouble – then the script of being in trouble is realized. Even if the tiniest thought of someone following you, flashes through your mind, a monster will start chasing you in your dream.

This happens because your soul instantly tunes into the variation that has just passed in your mind. *Your soul will choose a variation of the script that matches your thoughts and expectations.* The movement of the soul in the space of variations takes place at the same time as thoughts and expectations run through your head. Thoughts and expectations are actually the force that rolls the film reel. If one could stop the brain from working, then the viewed image would be frozen still. But thoughts do not stop and they are constantly spinning in our head.

Events taking place in a dream may be in conflict with standard beliefs, and this is because your mind's control is weaker when you are dreaming. All sorts of absurd and strange things happen to you in a dream, incredible visions appear before your eyes and the laws of physics are no longer working. Unbelievable things may happen in a lucid dream as well. After all, your mind understands that this is only a fantasy, and therefore it can allow any absurdity.

Now you see why everything is possible in a dream: *a dream is a soul's journey into the space of variations, and you can find any possible script in the space of variations.* This is the why in a lucid dream you are able to intentionally change the script of your dream. Actually, the script does not change – it is being chosen by your intention. As soon as the intention to swap roles with your persecutor enters your mind, your soul will switch over to a sector with the reverse script.

If the mind has realized that he can control what is happening, he will start formulating desires, like for instance, the desire to fly up in the air. This thought, having quickly flashed through your mind, will transform into intention in your soul. Intention is the moving force that transfers the dreamer into the sector with the corresponding script.

The journey of the soul in the space of variations is not burdened by the inertness of material objects. That is why dreams are so supple. The reserved script is immediately realized. And what happens in real life? Basically – the same thing. The only thing that differs is the speed with which the script is made into reality. In real life, events develop according to the same laws as the events that take place in dreams. However, they do not happen with the speed of lightning, because the material realization of variations has a certain degree of inertness. In this regard, the claim that our life is a dream is incorrect, but at the same time it is not deprived of logic. I have already illustrated how thoughts are able to shape events taking place in someone's life. What is on your mind now is what you will get sooner or later.

Your thoughts are a radiation of energy on the frequency of a particular life track. In real life, the transfer to this life track is slowed down by different material factors. A sector of space that has been realized in comparison to an unrealized one would appear sticky as tar when compared to water. Material manifestation of the potential variation occurs with a delay. There are no inert obstacles in a dream, and hence, the transfer between sectors is realized immediately.

At this point, it should be obvious to you why I started talking about dreams and dreaming. In order to rule our destiny, it is crucial for us to understand how our thoughts carry us from one sector to another and why not all of our desires are realized. However, in order to examine this question you don't have to get involved with lucid dreaming at all. Our goal is – to be able to choose a script when we are awake. *It is much more important to learn how to wake up in real life than in a virtual one.* Moreover, as I have already mentioned, there is certain danger associated with practicing lucid dreaming.

It is possible that those who practice lucid dreaming will tell you that there is nothing dangerous about it. However, they are probably unaware of the fact that they are walking on the edge of a razorblade. No one can guarantee that you will return from a lucid dream. While your soul is flying about in unrealized sectors – there is no danger. But what do you think will happen, when your soul will by chance get into a realized sector of space? The hypothesis is that you could materialize in that sector. We are all used to the fact that fantasies can be of no harm to us. Yet, as you see, the given assumption carries a threat. And what if it is a fact?

We know that ancient magicians, having fully mastered the art of dreaming, intentionally went away to other worlds to never come back. Their physical bodies disappeared from this world as well. Ancient magicians were either too reckless or knew too well what they were doing. In our times, every year there are *tens of thousands* of people disappearing without a trace. They simply vanish. There are even theories about alien abduction. I cannot say anything for sure, but it is possible that they simply do not return from their dreams. After all, a soul can fly into a realized sector even in an unconscious state.

Lucid dreaming is more dangerous in that sense, because your mind could lose his caution and fly into heaven knows where. No one can say whether you soul would be able to return. A physical body may even stay behind, and in that case, they would simply verify that death came in your sleep. It is not my aim to get you all scared. Just keep in mind that a dream is not an illusion. When having a lucid dream, you might be tempted to fool around a little bit. After all, you could do anything you wanted, and get away with it without causing any harm to other people. Or you could simply fly around and explore other worlds. Everything is allowed while your soul is in an unrealized virtual sector. Here is the dangerous part: there is no guarantee that your soul won't wander off to a sector that has already been realized. Your mind won't even be able to realize right away that virtual reality has turned into a physical one. Don't be under the delusion that our visible world is the only one in the Universe. The space of variations is infinite, and there are, of course, plenty of realized sectors in it, inhabited by all possible living beings.

The world, which you find yourself in, may be paradise in comparison to our world, but it may just as well be a living hell. The location of this world is also unknown. Maybe it is millions of light years away from our Earth, and maybe it is in your cup of coffee. That world could be very far away and, at the same time, it could be very close, but in another dimension. As previously mentioned in Chapter I, infinity stretches indefinitely only if you look straight ahead. But it does not matter whether that parallel world is far away or nearby, as it is very easy to get lost in it and extremely difficult to come back.

I won't touch upon the subject of astral journeys into the material world. There is a different mechanism at work, and the subject has nothing to do with Transurfing and it is a rather dangerous business all together. Generally speaking, dreams are only indirectly related to Transurfing. Our task is not to run away from the cruel reality into the bordering world of dreams, but to make our actual reality a more comfortable one.

There is no need to fear dreams, but one shouldn't take them lightly either. *If you feel discomfort in your soul when there is talk of lucid dreaming, then you shouldn't be doing it at all.* Your inner gut feeling should tell you whether something is dangerous for you or not. Your soul is better at sensing impending trouble, than your mind. Therefore, dreaming without the mind interfering is much safer. But if you have decided to give lucid dreaming a try after all, be careful and vigilant in your dream, don't push it and maintain a maximum awareness of what is going on. Just as in real life, feel yourself at home but don't forget that you are only a guest.

The Magic Power of Intention

So, we have established that our thoughts and desires direct our movement in the space of variations. In a dream, our movement is not slowed down by the inertness of material realization. The smallest whiff of thought instantly transports the dreamer into a sector of space. In realized sectors, things do not happen as quickly due to the heavy inertness of matter. However, the same principle is at work in our actual reality: our thoughts have a direct influence on the course of events in our life.

"Oh, really" – the Reader may ask with irony in their voice, that same Reader who is not yet completely confused by the wonders of this strange Transurfing model. – "And here I thought that it was not my thoughts but my actions that determined the course of my life. Silly me. Well, now, of course, I have been enlightened: the important thing is not what you do, but what you think."

Actually, there is nothing contradictory about this. And it doesn't even have anything to do with the fact that you think first and then act. People are used to paying attention to the consequences of their actions, because their actions are right there on the surface. The consequences of one's thoughts are many times not as obvious. This has to do with the action of balancing forces. We have already looked at examples where the activity of balancing forces turns out to be the opposite to that of a person's intention. In his attempt to get something, he gets the complete opposite. The greater the excess potential, the further away is his reality from his desired reality. He cannot find any explanation to why the world is behaving so strangely. Nonetheless, he tries to convince himself that he either did something wrong or such is the way of the world, or the desired can only be achieved with great difficulty.

It may seem that there is actually a contradiction in the model of Transurfing. On the one hand, it is being claimed that our thoughts modify the energy passing through us. This energy transfers people onto the life tracks that correspond to their thoughts. Or, as you now know, thoughts transfer us onto sectors of space with the corresponding script and decorations. This is exactly how things happen in a dream. Then, on the other hand, it turns out that our thoughts are of no greater significance in reality, because we cannot get the desired by simply thinking about it. No matter how much you think about what you want, while lying on a couch, a transfer to another life track won't happen, even if you were to take into account the inertness of material realization. "That is exactly the point – the pragmatic Reader will become animated. – I have to act! Thoughts and some kind of transfers have nothing to do with this." And he would be formally right.

But he will only be right formally. In reality, this contradiction only appears as such. We are getting closer to explaining why trying to visualize the desired is often fruitless. As you know, the first obvious reason has to do with excess potentials, which we create when trying to obtain the desired.

The second reason is the inertness of material realization of variations. Very often, we fail to reach our goal because we are not stubborn enough in our striving towards it. Many goals simply do not get the time to realize themselves, especially when you quickly grow cold towards your goal and give up on the "hopeless" case. You can probably even remember some situations in your life, when you got what you wanted but with a delay, when you have already lost all hope, and forgotten all about the order you've made.

Yet another typical mistake many people make is trying to get everything right away. If you have set many goals that are in no way connected to each other, then the whole of your mental energy will be in vain dispersed into emptiness. The flow of variations will not let you swim in different directions at the same time. Tuning into a specific sector will have a greater effect, when all your efforts are directed at one particular goal. We will return to this question in the next chapter.

None of the harmful factors mentioned above exist in a dream. Excess potentials are not in our way, inertness is not interfering, and even our mind is resting from the daily struggle of achieving goals. However, even in our dream all desires do not manage to come true. Those, who practice lucid dreaming, know that not every little thought transfers the dreamer into a corresponding sector. What, then, is the obstacle?

The answer is very simple and yet fundamental. There are no obstacles. And it has little to do with one's actual thoughts. The secret is that *it is not the desire itself that brings forth realization. Rather, it is you aiming at the desired.* It is not your actual thoughts about the desired object that make things happen, but something else instead – something that is difficult to put in words. This power is behind the scenes, while the play of thoughts occurs on stage. And yet, that power has the last word. You have, of course, already figured out that I am talking about *intention.* The mind was unable to find a suitable definition for intention, among all of his labels and files. We will roughly define intention as *the determination to have and to act.*

Now you understand that thoughts on their own do not really mean a thing in the process of tuning into a sector in the space of variations. Thoughts are just the foam on the crest of a wave. *Your intention is realized, not your desire.*

Let's once again look at the example where you are lifting your arm. Wish for your arm to lift. The desire has been formed in your thoughts: you are aware of the fact that you want to lift your arm. Does your desire lift your arm? No, your desire on its own does not create any action. Your arm will only be lifted when the thoughts about your desire have done their job and the only thing left is the determination to act. Perhaps it is the determination to act that lifts the arm? No, it doesn't. You have made the final decision to lift your arm, but it does not move. What then lifts the arm? How should we define what comes after determination? This is where we become aware of the fact that our mind is unable to clearly explain to us what intention really is. Our definition of intention as the determination to have and act, only demonstrates an introduction to the power that is actually responsible for any action. The only thing left for us to do is to state the following fact – an arm is lifted not with desire or determination, but with intention. I introduced the label "determination" only so that it would be easier to understand. But you, of course, are able to sense, no words necessary, that you possess a certain force that makes your muscles contract.

Actually, it is very difficult to explain what intention is. We do not wonder how to move our arms and legs, and we do not remember that we were once unable to walk. In the same way, a person does not yet know the right thing to do when he gets on the bike for the first time. But, even when he has learned how to ride a bike, he will not be able to explain how he does this. Intention is a very vague quality. It is hard to obtain, but it can also be easily lost. For example, someone who is paralyzed has no power of intention what so ever. The desire to move his legs is there, but the ability to translate this desire into action is absent. There are known cases, when paralyzed individuals began to walk under the influence of hypnosis or as a result of a miraculous recovery. Intention returned to them.

So, a desire on its own will take you nowhere. For example, the greater the desire, the more active the counteractive actions of balancing forces. Notice the following: the desire is directed at *the goal* itself, but intention is directed at *the process of reaching* that goal. Desire realizes itself by creating an excess potential of one's wish to reach the goal. Intention realizes itself by acting. Intention does not ponder on whether the goal is attainable or not. The decision has already been made, thus it only remains to act. If you want to fly in your dream, and if you are pondering on whether it is possible or not – you will get nowhere. In order to fly, you simply need to get yourself up in the air, using intention. *Choosing a script in a dream is not done with desire, but with a steady intent to get the desired. You are not contemplating and you do not desire. You are simply having and acting.*

We have already discussed the uselessness of desire. What about when you ask for something? There is nothing to say about that. There is no point in asking for something from the Guardian Angel, God, higher powers or any other powers. The laws of the Universe are absolutely dispassionate. No one needs your complains, hurt feelings and wailings. Gratitude – yes, because gratitude is by its nature close to unconditional love. True gratitude – it is *the radiation* of creative energy. The excessive potential of requests is the opposite – it is *a delay*, it is focusing energy on one spot only. Complains, requests and demands are the makings of pendulums, designed to harvest energy from people. Thoughts that are phrased in the following way – "give...to me" and "I want..." automatically create excessive potentials. You do not have the things you ask for, but you are trying to pull them towards you with your thoughts.

To ask something of higher or other powers is completely pointless. That is the same as going shopping and asking the clerk to give you the merchandise for free. You may ask of people, within reason of course, and if they are inclined to help you. Everything else in this world is built upon objective laws, and not on the desire to help someone.

Imagine the situation where Earth asks the Sun permission to transfer to another orbit. Absurd, isn't it? It is just as absurd to approach someone or something with a request, unless it is a human being. *The only thing that makes sense is to have the intention to choose.* You are really choosing your own destiny. If the parameters of your radiation correspond to your choice and no laws are being broken at the same time, then you will get what you want. *A choice is not a request - it is your determination to have and to act.*

Intention does not create excess potentials, because the energy of the potential created by desire is spent on action. *Desire and action are united in intention.* Intention in action naturally dissolves the excess potential that was created by your desire. This happens without the interference of balancing forces. When solving the problem – act. When pondering over how difficult the problem is, you are creating an excessive potential and at the same time you are giving energy away to a pendulum. When acting, you are realizing the energy of intention. There is a Russian saying "the eyes are fearing, but the hands are doing the job"[1]. Realizing your intention, trust the flow of variations, and the problem will be solved on its own.

Expectation, worry, excessive thinking and desires will only drain your energy. Intention in action will not only spend the energy of the potential, but it will bring it into the energetic membrane of a person as well. You can find proof of this in the example of learning. Cramming before exams takes a lot of effort and does not pay off. Yet, on the other hand, when you are actively studying, that is when you are doing practical work or solving problems, not only is it not exhausting but this way of studying brings you inspiration and satisfaction as well.

So, intention is the driving force that realizes sectors in the space of variations. But here is a question: why then do our fears get realized as well? Could they also be considered a part of our intention? It is the same way in real life, as it is in dreams –we are constantly being haunted by variations with scripts of our fears, worries, dislike and hate. After all, if I do not want something, I do not intend to have it, right? However, we still get what we actively do not want. So, turns out that the direction of our desires doesn't really matter? The key to this problem is hidden within an even more secret and powerful force, the name of which is – *external intention.*

External Intention

Intention is a combination of desire and action. Everyone is familiar with the intention of doing something with one's own powers. That is *internal intention.* It is much more difficult to extend the action of intention onto the outside world. That is *external intention.* With the help of external intention, you can rule the world. To be more exact, you will be able to choose the way the world around you will behave. You will be able to determine the script and decorations.

The concept of external intention is closely linked with the model of variations. All manipulations of time, space and matter, which cannot be explained logically, tend to be ascribed to magic or paranormal phenomena. And these phenomena actually demonstrate external intention at work – *external intention is directed at the process of choosing a life track in the space of variations.*

Internal intention is unable to turn an apple tree that you happen to see on your path into a pear tree. External intention does not *turn things into other things* either. Instead, it *chooses* a path with a pear tree instead of an apple tree in the space of variations, and completes the transfer. That is how an apple tree is replaced with a pear tree. Nothing actually happens to the apple tree – there is simply an exchange taking place: material realization moves in the space of variations from one track to another. No power is able to actually transform one object into another in some magical way – internal intention is aimed at doing that but its abilities are quite limited.

If you try to move a pencil with your mind – it won't move. But if you were to have a steady intention to imagine it moving, perhaps it would. Let's suppose that you were able to move the pencil (in any case, psychics are able to demonstrate some kind of results). What I am about to tell you next may seem very strange. Actually, the pencil does not move! And at the same time, if you manage to "move" the pencil, it would not be an illusion. In the first case, you are trying to move the pencil with the energy of your thoughts. There is obviously not enough of that energy to move material objects. In the latter case, you are sliding along the life tracks, where the pencil has different locations. Do you feel the difference?

The pencil is on the table. With the power of intention, you imagine how it starts to move. Your intention scans the sectors of space where the pencil has other, new locations. If your mental radiation is of adequate power, the pencil will materialize in the new locations, one after the other, in real space. At the same time, it is a separate "layer of the pencil" that is moving, while all other layers, including the layer of the observer remain static. *It is not the actual object that is moving, but rather the object's realization in the space of variation.*

It won't be a surprise if you won't be able to move the pencil at all. Almost everyone has very weak supernatural skills. And it is not that you have weak energy, but it is just very hard to believe that something like that is possible, and hence, it is very difficult to evoke pure intention in yourself. People gifted in telekinesis do not move objects. They possess a unique ability to direct their energy with the power of intention to move material realization in the space of variations.

Everything that is related to external intention is usually considered as mysticism, magic or, in the best cases, as unexplained phenomena, the testimonies and evidence of which are put on dusty shelves. The standard worldview completely rejects this kind of things. The irrational always evokes a peculiar fear. People that have seen an UFO experience a similar kind of fear and stupor. The unexplained phenomenon is so far away from the reality we are used to that we do not want to believe that it is possible. And yet, it has such an astounding audacity to be real that it provokes horror.

External intention is when "if Mohammed does not go to the mountain, then the mountain goes to Mohammed". And you thought it was just a joke? The workings of external intention are not necessarily followed by paranormal phenomena. We are constantly facing the results of the actions of external intention in everyday life. Our fears and worst expectations in particular are realized by external intention. But since external intention in this case is operating independently of our will, we are not aware of how it all happens. It is much harder to control external intention than to control inner intention.

Imagine that you disembark on an island, and there you meet savages. Now your life depends on your behavior. First option: you are a victim. You apologize, offer gifts, you make excuses and ingratiate yourself with the savages. In this case, your lot is to be eaten. Second option: you are the conqueror. You act aggressively, attack and try to subdue the savages. Your lot is to either conquer or perish. Third option: you present yourself as the master, the ruler. You extent your hand, as the all ruling hand - and people obey you. If you have no doubts about your might, then others will also think that it could not be in any other way. Your mental radiation is tuned into the life tracks where you are a ruler.

The first two options are related to the activity of inner intention, but the third option demonstrates the action of external intention. External intention simply chooses the needed variation.

The fly that is beating against the glass, when there is an open window nearby, has inner intention. What do you think would be external intention to this fly? There is an obvious answer – to fly out the open window, but that is not it. If the fly were to fly back and look around, it would notice the closed window glass and the open window. The fly would then just have a wider perspective on reality. External intention in its pure form opens the closed window before the fly.

Internal intention has to do with any attempt to influence the world around you on one and the same life track. Everything that is possible within the borders of *a separate sector* in the space of variations is described by well-known natural laws and fits the material worldview. External intention is a part of any attempt to choose a life track, where the desired is realized.

It must be evident to you by now, that to fly through a closed window would be an example of internal intention. External intention, on the other hand, would be to transfer onto a life track where the window is opening. One could put inhuman efforts into trying to move the pencil with the power of one's mind. Alternatively, one could scan the space of variations with different locations of the pencil by using one single external intention.

Let us suppose that you are sure of the fact that you won't be able to find a parking space by the supermarket the day before Christmas. Your inner intention claims: where would you get a parking space at this time? After all, everyone is busy shopping. External intention, on the other hand, assumes that you drive up to the supermarket and at that moment, a parking space is freed up just for you. It is not even the case that external intention steadily and firmly believes in such a possibility – it just *dispassionately and unconditionally takes what belongs to it.*

External intention is something that is created in improvisation, much like irradiation. It is pointless trying to prepare for external intention. All magic rituals are aimed at summoning one's own external intention. But a ritual is only a preparation for the magic, a theatrical prelude, a decoration. Imagine that you are flying off a cliff in your dream, and in order to not hit the ground you must summon the intention to levitate. There is no time to prepare or to utter spells. Just intend to fly and it will happen. Spells and magical attributes only help to awaken the power that each person has but is unable to use.

Unfortunately, the ability to control external intention is almost non-existent in the modern man. People even managed to completely forget about the fact that they once had that ability. Only in ancient legends is this information vaguely mentioned. Now, you don't even need to bother trying to prove that the Egyptian pyramids and other similar constructions were built with the help of external intention. All possible hypotheses will be accepted except this one. It seems to me that the builders of the pyramids would be quite amused to hear that their descendants, who believe that their ancestors are of a backward civilization, will bend over backwards in their attempts to unravel their mystery within the limits of internal intention.

But people are not completely derived of external intention. It is just that their external intention is tightly blocked. All what is usually considered to be magic is nothing more than people trying to work with external intention. For centuries, alchemists have been unsuccessful in trying to find the philosopher's stone that would turn any object into gold. Many intricate books that are hard to understand have been dedicated to the subject of alchemy. But in reality, as the legend reads, the secret of the philosopher's stone fits within a few lines, carved on an emerald plate – the so called Emerald Tablet. Why then all these books? They were probably written to understand these few lines.

You have almost certainly heard about the Holy Grail. Many have been actively searching for it, even the representatives of the Third Reich. There are always legends of similar items that allegedly grant unlimited might and power. These are naive delusions. No object is able to give you any power. Fetishes, spells and other things have no power on their own. The power is within the external intention of those that make use of these things. Paraphernalia is only able to help the subconscious to a certain extent, activating the dormant and underdeveloped seeds of external intention. Believing that certain things possess magic power gives an impulse that awakens external intention.

Ancient civilizations achieved such levels of perfections that they could do without the magic rituals. Of course, possessing such a power created an extremely strong excess potential. Therefore, civilizations alike Atlantis that opened the secrets of external intention were from time to time destroyed by balancing forces. The shards of this esoteric knowledge have reached our times in the shape of magic practices, the goal of which is to restore what was lost. However, these are only weak and superficial attempts that are walking on the wrong path, that of internal intention. The essence of might and power – external intention – remains a mystery.

Pendulums are responsible for the preferred development of internal intention and the loss of external intention in people. And this is simply because they feed on the energy of internal intention. Controlling external intention is only possible when you are completely independent from pendulums. One could say that in this case they have gained a definitive victory in the battle with man.

So, we have found out that the nature of mental energy that is aimed at attaining a goal can be manifested in three different forms: desire, internal intention and external intention. *Desire is focusing attention on the goal itself.* As you can see, desire has no power. You could think about the goal and desire it all you want, but nothing will change because of that. *Internal intention is focusing on the process of one's movement towards the goal.* That is already working, but it does take a lot of effort. *External intention is focusing on how the goal is realized by itself.* External intention simply *allows* the goal to be realized on its own. At the same time, it is implied that you have a fixed conviction that a variation of the realized goal exists already and you only have to choose it. *The goal is attained by internal intention, while external intention chooses the goal.*

Internal intention could be described by the following formula: "I insist that..." External intention follows a completely different rule: "The circumstances are such that..." or "It turns out that..." The difference is huge. In the first case, you are actively acting upon the world so that it would yield to you. In the second case, you are assuming the position of an outside observer – everything happens according to your will, but it kind of happens on its own. You do not change things – you choose them instead. Flying in a dream happens according to this specific formula: "It turns out that I am flying", and not "I insist that I fly".

Internal intention is - aiming for *the goal* directly, regardless of any obstacles. External intention is aimed at *the process of independent realization of the goal.* External intention is not in a rush to reach the goal – the goal is already in your pocket. The fact that the goal will be reached is beyond any doubts and is not subject to discussion. External intention is inexorably, coolly, dispassionately and unavoidably moving the goal towards realization.

In order to distinguish between your internal intention and external intention at work, use two sided comparisons that go something like this: you're trying to get something from this world – it gives you what you want; you are fighting for a place under the sun – the world is opening its arms to you; you are trying to break through a close door – the door is opening on its own, right in front of you; you are trying to force your way through a wall – the wall parts in front of you; you are trying to call forth certain events in your life – they come on their own. Basically, by using internal intention you are trying to move your realization in relation to the space of variations, and external intention moves the space of variation in such a way that your realization winds up in the right place. Can you see the difference? The result is the same, but the paths leading to the result are completely different.

If your actions can be described using the second part of these comparisons, then you have captured external intention. When you are struggling, you are trying to push your realization in the space of variations, but when you are choosing, the space of variations is moving towards you. Obviously, the space of variations won't be moving on its own relative to your realization. In order for that to happen, you must take certain actions. Yet, these actions are outside the limits of ordinary and general conceptions. Throughout this book I will provide examples of differences in the approaches of internal and external intention. External intention is a cornerstone of Transurfing. Within external intention lies the key to the Riddle of the Overseer, which is the reason to why you do not need to struggle with this world, and instead simply choose what you want.

There is nothing impossible for external intention. You could fly even in real life or, say, walk on water, if you have the external intention of Christ. No physical laws would be broken. The thing is that physical laws work in one single and separate sector of material realization. The activity of external intention appears in the movement of realization along the different sectors of the space of variations. Within the limits of one realized sector – flying is impossible. To fly, you would need to counteract the gravity of the Earth, and that is the job of internal intention, which requires a certain amount of energy to be spent in order to overcome gravity. Free flying, both in a dream or in real life - is not your actual movement in the physical space, but rather a change in the location of your realization. In other words, your body is being materialized at new points in the material space along a certain direction.

It would also be possible to say that *you are not flying through the space on your own, but the space is moving in relation to you and in accordance with the choice of your external intention.* Most likely, that is not the most correct way to put it, but we won't be getting further into the theory of relativity. We can only guess how it all actually happens.

To fly, you need to have an unreserved belief that it is something that is possible to do. Why did Christ say the following in such a peremptory and simple way "According to your faith will it be done to you"[2]? It is because we are unable to get or do anything without having any intention. And there is no intention without faith. We wouldn't even be able to take a step, if we didn't believe that it was possible. However, you won't be able to convince your mind, at least in its normal state, that one can fly in real life just like one can in a dream. Some yogis in India, while being in the process of mediation, manage to get their bodies off the floor. (I personally do not know of any other reliable manifestations of levitation.) It is possible that their intention is barely enough to tune into the movement of variations, where the body is hovering in the air. Taking into account the immense abilities of yogis in comparison with ordinary people, you can probably imagine how hard it is to submit external intention to your will.

While you are dreaming, the dozing mind is still able to admit that flying is possible, but when you are awake, flying is something inconceivable to your mind, despite any persuasions on your part. There has to be knowledge – not simply faith. Faith implies a possibility of doubt. Where there is faith there is also doubt. Knowledge excludes doubt. You have no doubts that the apple you just dropped will fall onto the ground, do you? You do not believe it will happen, you just know. Pure external intention is free of doubt, and hence of faith. If, in order to fly in a dream, a hint of external intention is enough, then in the world of inert material realization intention must be absolutely pure. But do not let the impossibility to obtain pure intention upset you. To realize your goal it is quite enough with a "second class" intention. It will just take a certain amount of time for the inert realization to "properly untwist".

In the context of external intention arises an interesting question: what is hypnosis? I cannot say for sure whether hypnosis is a product of internal or external intention. There is clearly not enough mental energy to move even the lightest of objects with the power of internal intention. However, that energy is quite enough to allow for the transfer of different suggestions from one person to another. Some people demonstrate highly pronounced abilities in directing a rather powerful energy stream. If the stream is modified by certain thoughts then the person, at whom this stream was aimed, will experience an effect of suggestion. I hope you don't think that the hypnotizer operates merely through the means of a magnetic gaze or random arm movements. Especially since affecting someone energetically does not always require visual or auditory contact. However, as far as I know, hypnosis works mostly at close distances. Then it is only natural to assume that hypnosis is a product of mental energy transfer, which is done by internal intention. In those cases, when hypnosis works at great distances, external intention undeniably plays the main part, unless there are some other mechanisms at work.

In order to experience external intention, you must break free from the Procrustean bed of the usual conceptions and feelings. Mind exists within the narrow limits of the conventional worldview. To escape beyond these limits is difficult because such an escape can only be done with the help of external intention. The mind will not give up its positions so easily. So, it becomes a vicious circle: you need external intention in order to grasp external intention. That is the whole difficulty of it.

I am afraid I'll disappoint some readers by saying that I do not know of any exercises that develop and strengthen external intention. The goal of such exercises would perhaps go something like this: "gather intention to have intention". The only option that allows one to get a deeper understanding of the nature of external intention is the practice of lucid dreaming. In real life, however, instead of exercises, I can offer the practice of lucid living. That does not mean so much to practice, but to live through external intention. Reality differs from a dream only in its inertness of material realization in the space of variations. Everything else is the same.

You could ask a question: if we are not able to control external intention then what can we rely on? Obviously, you probably won't be able to move blocks that weigh several tons. But the inertness of the material world can be overcome through time. The conventional and most common way of reaching goals is based on internal intention. The essence of Transurfing is in doing the opposite – rejecting internal intention and using external intention instead.

It is hard to draw a line between where internal intention ends and external intention starts. Internal intention turns into external when your consciousness is united, coordinated and merged with the subconscious. This line is imperceptible. It is similar to the sensation of a free fall or that feeling when you first managed to ride a two-wheeled bicycle. But it is probably explained best by the sensation of flying in your dream, when you are intentionally getting yourself up in the air.

Your consciousness is amalgamated and is wholly coordinated with your subconscious in a specific narrow segment. It is easy for you to move your fingers, a little harder to move your toes, even harder to move your ears, and almost impossible to move your inner organs. External intention is even less developed. To unite consciousness and unconsciousness in the intention to lift off the ground and fly is so difficult that it is regarded as being practically impossible.

We will be setting more down-to-earth kind of goals. Levitation is the greatest manifestation of pure external intention. But the power of external intention is so great that even the smallest piece of external intention would be enough to get some impressive results. In everyday life, eternal intention is working regardless of our will and it often has a harmful effect. For example, external intention could be manifested through the realization of our worst fears. We have already discussed situations, where a person gets what he does not want. On the one hand, things that you fear, hate and want to escape are following you. This happens because your mental radiation, being tuned into an unwanted event, transfers you to the sector where this event is taking place. But on the other hand, you do not intend to have what you do not want, do you? Where is then the work of intention in a situation like that?

Internal intention is aimed at escaping the unwanted. All those things that worry you, that you fear and loathe, hit your soft spots. You want to escape them with all your heart. The mind is afraid – the soul is even more afraid, the mind feels loathing – the soul does not have anything against loathing either, the mind hates – the soul hates even more. The soul and mind are completely unanimous. External intention is awakened in the exact moment when your consciousness and your subconscious are synchronized. Yet, that kind of external intention is not directed at what you need. It wouldn't even be right to talk about the direction of your intention. If internal intention has an exact direction – to escape the unwanted, then external intention is probably not indicating a direction, but *a green light for the realization of whatever the soul and mind have agreed upon.* And they agree upon one thing – the evaluation of the event. Whether it is a desired or an unwanted event – doesn't matter. External intention sees the unanimity of the soul and mind, and simply chooses the corresponding sector in the space of variations.

Unfortunately, in life the soul and mind are most often unified in what they do not want or accept. Therefore, the realization of our worst fears is the most characteristic illustration of external intention's activity. People usually have a vague idea about what they want with all their heart, but they know very well what they really want to avoid. In order to submit external intention to your will, it is necessary to achieve agreement between the soul and mind in positive aspirations, and throw all negative thoughts away. You already know what a harmful effect a negative attitude can have on our life. When expressing dissatisfaction and non-acceptance, you are subject to the actions of balancing forces, you develop dependence on destructive pendulums and you direct your mental radiation at negative sectors of space. External intention, shaped by the negative, makes the negative your reality.

Thereby, external intention is able to act in spite of your will. To master this major force is difficult, but you can make it work for you and not against you. We shall dedicate ourselves to the solution of this particular problem. We already know what we should do in order to escape any harmful effect of external intention - you should not create excess potentials, and you should reject the negative. It remains to discuss what we need to do to make external intention serve our goal. That is not as easy as rubbing Aladdin's lamp, but there are methods that are helpful in setting the mechanism of external intention in motion.

It may be that most of the above information remains unclear to you. It is truly a difficult topic to grasp, as external intention cannot be described with words. However, you will soon get a clear picture of it all. I have no desire to fog and confuse you, in order to get you interested, as followers of some schools and spiritual movements love doing. All that is necessary for you to know is in this book. All that is necessary for you to know how to do, you will get from your own experience, if you will put the principles of Transurfing to practice. No special exercises or training will be required. There is nothing mystical or secret about Transurfing.

"Esoteric knowledge" is usually encircled by indirectness and omissions. Yet, everyone knows that he who reasons clearly is also clear in his communication. And if someone who has this "esoteric knowledge" wants to show that he knows something extraordinary, something that he can supposedly only tell his apprentice in secret, so that no one else would hear, while all the other time he is expressing himself with ambiguity and thoughtful sentences, then most probably this guru does not have a clear idea himself of what the core of his knowledge is.

We will not try to obtain an absolute intention that would be able to get a body in the air. If I knew how to do that, then we would have nothing more to discuss. There is the space of variations, there is the possibility of choice – choose your variation, period. Our task is to learn how to achieve a goal using our own abilities. Even with all the limitations of our abilities, Transurfing provides knowledge that can awaken powers that we do not use. And for that to happen, one does not need to exhaust oneself with meditations, trainings, lucid dreaming and other mystical practices, which may cause you to lose it. The model of Transurfing appears, of course, to be incredible. It is really difficult to believe in all this. Nonetheless, should you only review your views on life that you are accustomed to; you would be able to achieve what previously seemed to be unachievable. Soon you shall see for yourself: you can actually make external intention work for you.

The Script of the Game

Let's once again return to dreams and dreaming. Dreams are very plastic, and therefore serve as an excellent demonstration model for understanding the mechanism behind external intention. We have already seen that the nature of dreams is in many ways similar to real life. Everything that happens in a dream is a result of a game that occurs according to a script chosen by our soul. When the mind is sleeping, we watch dreams, but we do not remember them. In a case like that, the soul is traveling in the space of variations without any control. Where the soul is gadding about at times like this - nobody knows. All our conscious memories are under our mind's control. Dreams that we do remember, occur when our mind is drowsing. At times like this, the mind's control is weaker, and hence, the mind plays the part of a passive observer. The mind is not imagining anything, and he does not think he is seeing something that is not there. The mind perceives whatever the soul is seeing in the unrealized sectors of the space of variations.

In an unconscious dream, the mind does not dominate the soul with its control. The mind is watching a movie, just like a viewer would. And at the same time, the mind is going through whatever it is it saw, and these experiences are passed on to the soul. The soul then immediately tunes into a sector that corresponds to the expectations. This way, the script is changing dynamically, during the course of events. Decorations and characters are instantly adjusted to fit the constantly changing script. Imagination is actually involved in a dream, but it works only as a generator of ideas.

This is what happens in a dream: a fleeting thought that someone is aggressively disposed towards you passed through your mind, and that thought is instantly materialized - that person starts threatening you. But as soon as the weather vane of your opinion has bent to the other side - the enemy immediately turns into a friend. A kitten behaves the same way in front of a mirror – his mood swings from friendly to aggressive. He sees a subject in front of him, and so he starts evaluating what he could expect from such a fellow. At first, his attitude is neutral – he is curious. But now he is lifting his paw, his evaluation is immediately leaning towards the side of potential danger, the kitten is bristling up, attacking and defending. Then he jumps back and sees his own comical figure. His mood changes to playful. And after that, it starts all over again. Thus, a kitten is dynamically adjusting his own script. One moment he is attacking his mirror image, and then suddenly aggression is replaced with friendliness.

In an unconscious dream, you are correcting your script in the same way. The kitten is not aware of that he is looking at his mirror image, and you are not aware of that you are watching a dream. But do you know that we all look in the mirror with a different face expression than the one we usually have? The expression on your face changes immediately, just as soon as you glance at a mirror. The change happens instantaneously, we do not even notice it. This is because we have early on developed a habit of doing so and because we wish to look a certain way. Should one only say to a child: "Look in the mirror – your face is not at all pretty when you are crying" – the expression on the child's face will change at once. Grown ups are also looking at their mirror image with a certain expectation, for example: "I like myself", "How do I look?", "I don't like myself" or something else. But in any case, the look on a person's face is immediately adjusted.

The mirror is an example of dynamic adjusting of a script. Only here, it is internal intention at work. However, when you are dreaming it is external intention that is responsible for that very same action. When you are awake, you see your reflection in the mirror and immediately change your facial expression according to your expectations. Your facial expression is changed by your internal intention. *A person sees a game in their dream, while their external intention, regardless of their will, chooses the behavioral script of the surrounding world in accordance with their feelings and expectations.*

The behavior of the people in your dream is completely determined by your ideas of how they could be behaving themselves. An idea is only the first push; everything else is done by external intention. Your behavior in your dream is determined by internal intention, everything else obeys your external intention, whether you want it or not. As you remember, internal intention attempts to *affect* the outside world directly, while external intention – *allows* the outside world to realize itself in accordance with your intention.

In a dream, events develop only according to a script you can conceive of. Nothing could happen that would be beyond your comprehension. This explains the low level of critical evaluation of everything that happens in a dream. Even the most absurd things are taken for granted by the dreamer, and this is because that person is the scriptwriter and the director of his own dreams. Not that absurdity would be something that occurs every single time, but their potential possibility is not ruled out by the subconscious. After all, the rational mind is drowsing when you are dreaming, and thus the subconscious could very well allow for various incredible things to happen.

Throughout your life, a lot of external information but also information from your fantasies and imagination passes through your brain. A part of that information is filtered out by the rational mind as being defective and unreal. However, that part does not go anywhere. Even though the rejected information is in a cellar with a lock on, the subconscious still has access to that information. In addition, the subconscious has no reason to throw that information in the defective pile. Thus, when it is time to have a dream, the soul tiptoes to the cellar and starts trying on various absurd scripts in secret without the mind's knowledge. In addition, when you are having an unconscious dream, the soul is free to choose any sector of the space of variations. Most of these sectors will never be realized, as the events occurring in these sectors are irrational, and thus demand a lot of energy. God only knows how the soul picks her dreams.

No matter how frivolous the soul is in choosing her dreams, the mind sees them and adjusts the script in accordance with his feelings and expectations. As we have already clarified, our worst fears and all those things we are trying to avoid are realized most easily. In that case, external intention is working in spite of your will and to your detriment.

So, the scripts of our dreams are determined by our expectations. Worst fears or expectations are definitely realized in a dream. In real life, it is also more probable that you will get what you fear and do not want. This is how external intention works in spite of the will of the mind. By using his willpower, the mind is able to make internal intention work. External intention, however, does not follow orders. It manifests at its own choosing, as a product of agreement between your soul and mind. When dreaming, the mind doesn't even have the possibility to understand that external intention is at work, because he is no longer in control. Things are not much better in real life, because the dream in some sense continues when you are awake.

A person could be involved in the most absurd and meaningless games in a dream. The game absorbs the dreamer completely, and he does not realize how absurd everything really is. In real life, the same thing is happening to a lesser or greater extent. If a group of people are working in a highly specialized field, then it often happens that opinions, certain vocabulary and actions are formed that might seem completely absurd and unnatural to an outsider. These may be groups of people sharing the same interests or ideas, like professional or religious groups.

Having low critical assessment of everything that happens when you are awake gives rise to such phenomena as hypnosis and entrancement. For example, gypsy hypnosis is based on three "yes". A person answers three questions with a "yes", and he is under the illusion that everything is as it should be. He is no longer on his guard and it is almost as if he falls asleep – his ability to critically asses the situation goes down. Quite a lot of people are almost literally sleeping, while they are up and about, doing things automatically, things they are used to do every day. This concerns those people in particular, who have the same routine day in and day out.

When you are talking to someone, you are sleeping very soundly. When you are plunging into a game, you, obviously, understand what is going on, but you are unable to asses the situation or to act objectively. This is because you are not watching the game from the outside, but you are actually taking part in it. A soccer fan is knowingly criticizing the players for making mistakes. And what would happen if this fan was let out on the soccer field? All people are to some extent acting unconsciously. If a person is not telling the truth, his eyes will tend to shift to the right. His arms are making involuntary and uncontrolled movements. This person is completely in the power of the play he is acting in.

The state of hypnotic suggestion is the utmost level of sleeping awake. Everyone, to some extent, continues to sleep in his or her real life. Now, you could rouse yourself and say: I am aware of what I am doing and what is happening this very moment. But then you will get distracted by a person, a problem or an event, and you will plunge into the game and fall asleep. And you will sleep, while you are on stage and are playing your role voluntarily. You will wake up once you step down to the auditorium and give your Watcher a push. While you are in the auditorium, you will continue to play your part, saying the necessary words, doing what's required, obeying the set rules. Only now, you will play consciously, and that means – playing in a detached way. You are renting yourself out, and you sensibly evaluating what's going on.

In an unconscious dream, the dream just "happens" to you - external intention acts regardless of your will and you can't do anything about it. In a lucid or conscious dream, you step down from the stage to the auditorium and deliberately manage the script. It is not that external intention bends to your will; rather it simply does not go against it. In that case, your mind gives the soul her liberty and gets the soul's agreement in return. The unity of the soul and mind awakens external intention. In the upcoming chapters, we are going to discuss how to obtain this unity on the way to you goal.

In real life, the level of awareness is higher than in a dream.

This is quite enough in order to control internal intention. External intention, however, requires an even higher level of awareness. It is the same in real life, as it is in lucid dreaming, *in order to get control over external intention you have to wake up.*

The Game According to Your Rules

What would you do if someone was attacking you in your dream? There are four options of internal intention: to run away, to fight, to wake up or to realize that you are awake. Resisting an attack or retreating in a dream is a primitive reaction of internal intention. If you have been attacked, and you are trying to defend yourself and resist the attack, then everything will happen in roughly the same way as it would in real life that is according to the usual model. There is a script in your consciousness that describes how a struggle should occur. For example, if you are used to losing, then you will lose. Your dream will move in the space of variations according to that script.

You act in a dream just as you are used to act in real life. Since everything is possible in a dream, it would be much more efficient to make use of external intention. You could calmly turn towards the enemy and with a little bit of willpower imagine that person self-destructing or turning into, say, a frog. In this case, you are not actually striving to *turn* him into a frog. Trying to affect the outside world is the job of internal intention. You are imagining that person *transforming*, in other words, you allow for the existence of such a variation. *Internal intention is only aimed at imagining such a situation, at allowing for a script like that.* If your mind completely allows for events to develop in this way, then the soul won't have any objections either. The unity of your soul and mind gives rise to external intention, and it realizes the chosen script.

As you can see, *external intention does not appear as a result of your willpower but as a product of the unity between soul and mind.* Internal intention (your will) must only be aimed at achieving this unity. In this sense, external intention is not a product of your will and somehow it functions independently of your will. But in order for external intention to appear, it is necessary to *realize* that you can control the script. Awareness is a vital condition, if you want to make external intention work for you.

A dream is not under any control when it is an unconscious dream – the dream just "happens". Most of your actions are relatively unconscious when you are dreaming but also when you are awake. Being unaware of what is going on is experiencing a situation as something determinable, and as something that is caused by external factors. Most of the time, you are unable to influence these factors to any significant degree due to a lack of power or means. If you hold such an opinion, then your life is usually influenced by other people or by vicissitudes of fate. In that sense, reality "happens" to you as well. The rules of the game are not set by you, but by the outside world.

In order to gain control over your dreams, as well as over your life, you need to switch from the role of a participant onto the role of an observer. Meanwhile, don't stop participating in the role playing game and continue to play your part just as before. But your inner Watcher should always be active. It is as if you are renting yourself out as an actor and, at the same time, you are watching your own performance and the performance of others in a detached way, as a viewer sitting in the auditorium. The Watcher is always on in the background. He doesn't interfere, but he keeps note and is highly aware of everything that is going on.

In a passive dream, the observer is off and there is only the actor. You are completely absorbed by your part and you do not see the situation from the outside. Do not get too engrossed with your role. It is crucial to maintain the internal and external importance at a minimal level. Always have your Watcher ready. Even if one were to disregard from external intention, your ability to control the situation is directly proportional to your awareness. In a dream, the level of your awareness is low and that is why a dream is something that "happens" to you. If you, however, have realized that you are sleeping, the entire situation gets under your control. You do whatever you want.

How susceptible you are to the influence of others and to the influence of destructive pendulums is inversely proportional to awareness. In a dream, many people act as zombies. If you are being pursued by a nightmare, you are running away and can't do anything about it. The script is yours, but you gave it away to another director for production. You are held captive by your own ideas about possible ways of how events might develop. They are your ideas, but they dictate their will, and thus you are but an actor that is a victim.

Remember this mechanism when you immerse yourself into a problem of some kind. For example, a colleague comes up to you and tells you that some task needs to be done. If it is somehow a problem for you then your first reaction would be worry, if not a depressing feeling. Several scripts of how things might develop are instantly played in your head: "This is a difficult job to do. How do I go about completing it? Oh, I really don't want to! What a troubled and difficult life I live. If I do not do this job then…", and so on. That is it, in that moment you've got involved in the game. You've got under the influence of pendulums or, to put it differently, you fell asleep. Now you are like an obedient child, who can be simply taken by the hand, and led into a room where a difficult and burdensome task is already waiting. You are now on a life track, where that is really the case.

And this happened only because you've allowed pendulums to hypnotize you and to force on you their game of problems. Having played the "problematic" script in your consciousness, you've coordinated your soul and mind in your anxiety, and so external intention instantly transferred you to the "problematic" life track. That is not difficult at all, as such feelings like fear, despair, dissatisfaction, worry and anxiety can easily come over us. And what caused it all in the first place? Importance! You've been dragged into a game, or put to sleep, only because you've evaluated the game as important on its own and important to you. That is both external and internal importance.

Now imagine another way of how these events might develop. Somebody approaches you with a problem. Rouse yourself and tell yourself that you are not asleep and that you can decide for yourself whether the first push of a pendulum will turn into a problem for you or not. Now you only have to fulfill the second condition: get the intention to make the pendulum fall through. Even when you do not know what lies ahead, decide for yourself in advance to view the situation as a mere trifle. The main thing is to keep anyone or anything from taking you by the hand and leading you someplace. Do not undertake any offensive actions, do not say no, do not try to get out of the situation and, what is even more important, - do not get irritated. Just calmly listen to the person and to whatever it is he wants you to do. It is advisable if you on the surface nod and say yes, however inside - you should be an outside observer, and not a participant. That is the role of a viewer playing a part and it could be likened to a football coach playing football.

To be detached in this case does not mean that you should be absent minded. It is rather the opposite, having the situation under control implies attention and complete clarity of thought. Standing on the sideline means to be aware of that you are the one setting the rules of the game and that you decide whether the game will turn into a tragedy or into a comic sketch. Well, and what do you want yourself? You probably want everything to be resolved nicely and smoothly. If you think that there will always be a difficult problem requiring a lot of effort, then you needn't worry. There is a simple solution to any difficult problem. This solution lies on the "comedy" life track. *To transfer to this life track, you will only need the intention to imagine that everything will be this way.*

Having applied this method you will be pleasantly surprised. The outcomes might be of the most incredible nature. At the very least, your problem will be solved very easily. Or perhaps the problem will simply be dropped or its solution will be someone else's responsibility. After all, there are simply no difficult problems on the "comedy" life track. You do not have any power over external intention, but by using the above method, you would be acting in a way that A - wouldn't turn external intention against you, and B - would get you a chance to make external intention work for your benefit. The circumstances may be very different or even unfavorable to you personally. However, assuming a position like that will dramatically increase your chances of winning. At the same time, do not forget to trust the flow of variations. If the soul and mind are sufficiently united in their "comedy" attitude towards the problem, then you will get astonishing results of which you could never dream before.

You are no longer a string puppet. I must only warn you of the temptation to imagine yourself being the puppet master. You realize that such an attitude would disturb the balance, and you would certainly get a flick on the nose, once the first signs of conceit or (God forbid!) resentment towards other people emerge. You will never get absolute and full control over everything that happens, not even in your dreams. Remember, *you have only the right to choose, and not to change.* Feel yourself at home, but do not forget that you are only a guest. You should also keep the following in mind: when you are renting yourself out, act irreproachably. *Having a "comic" attitude to the problem is not slacking or being careless, it is rather a sensible evaluation of importance.*

It would be a mistake to interpret awareness as a desire to establish control over the surrounding world. The mind is used to having its way, trying to alter the course of events, in other words, fighting the flow. If you have gone down to the auditorium, you might be tempted to change the script by force, trying to impose your will on the actors. Such behavior has nothing to do with Transurfing, as it rests solely on the internal intention of fighting the flow. Remind yourself again and again that you need to move with the flow of variations. *Awareness is not about control but about observation.* Control is only aimed at avoiding wallowing in the negative, and instead imagining a pleasant script, letting it into your life and accepting it with your whole heart. *Do not impose your script on the world. Allow for the possibility where the world is letting that particular variation realize itself. Allow yourself to have that variation. You will stop fighting the world, and only once your soul and mind are unite will you be able to let yourself choose.*

Let's recall that homework that was given to you in the previous chapter. The roles of the Asker, the Offended and the Warrior do not suit us. What role would Transurfing give someone who wants to be a master of his own life in this game called Life? It should be obvious to you by now that it is the *role of the Overseer*. The higher the level of your awareness when you are awake, the more efficient you will be at mastering your fate.

The role of the Overseer is, in addition, by far more interesting than the role of the Performer. As you know, commanders, chiefs and other leaders have a more active life position than ordinary performers. Leaders are rather overseers than someone who is carrying out duties. Their status obliges them to be "more awake" in comparison to the common workers, who can sleep while forcedly doing what is required of them. Having assumed the position of an Overseer, you will immediately feel a rush of energy. Your vigor will increase as well, because now you would no longer have to get depressed while fulfilling someone else's will, you would be creating your own fate instead. *Being responsible for your fate is not a burden – it is freedom.*

Man differs from animals, not as much because of his intellect but more due to his degree of awareness. Animals are in a more sleepy state. Their behavior is primarily determined by innate stereotypical scenarios, which emerge as instincts and reflexes. Animals act as if they were acting in a play, following a script that cannot be changed. A person is, in that sense, "more awake". They are more naturally aware of themselves as an individual and of their place in this world. And yet, the degree of a person's awareness is still very low. Man is playing his game, while still being on stage. He is completely absorbed by this game.

The secret of so-called intelligent people lies in their awareness. Clarity of mind is determined by the level of awareness. Some people think clearly and are able to articulate their thoughts in a clear way - others have a mess in their head. A sharp intellect on one side, and stupidity on the other – are not in the least degrees of intellectual development, they are different levels of awareness. Stupidity is rather a psychological shield, defending a person from unwanted information: "I don't want to know anything! Leave me alone already!" A sharp mind is exactly the opposite – openness, curiosity, the desire to obtain and process information: "I want to know everything!" Stupidity is sometimes a product of dormancy. Both qualities may be developed in childhood, for example, when parents, teachers and so on force the child to study something, while putting the child under a lot of psychological pressure at the same time.

The heavier we sleep while we are awake, the more mistakes we make. The fly that is beating against the glass is sleeping just as heavily. Immersing yourself in a game does not allow you to take a broad and objective view on things. Obsession with a game narrows your focus of perception and puts a screen in front of you. Therefore, when a person is making mistakes because of his obsession with the game, he later wonders: "Where was I looking?" As if he experienced a delusion. Even when it is the 1st of April (April Fools' Day), and the person knows that someone might play a joke on him, he still falls into the trap. Isn't that sleeping awake?

To a varying degree, unawareness sets in when a person does not want to face reality. The desire to walk away from the impending reality, forces the ostrich to hide its head in the sand. This tendency appears in a man's attempt to isolate himself from the world: "I don't see anything, I don't hear anything, I don't want anything, so leave me alone!" It is not possible to completely bury oneself under the covers and fall asleep. So, this person unwillingly attempts to block his perception, thus lowering his degree of awareness. For example, a non-aggressive and harmless person is trying to cover himself from an inevitable blow. But he is unable to ward off this blow, because his awareness is blocked by fear and his reaction is slowed down – as if his eyes have been clouded. Fury clouds one's comprehension in the same way. The person is entirely immersed in the game and doesn't see or hear anything. Hence, the expression "blind fury".

Fear and fury are the extreme manifestations of unawareness. Pendulums all around us are trying to softly lull our vigilance to sleep. Advertisement, for example, has a zombifying effect, exploiting the fact that people are spending the majority of their time half-aware of what is going on around them. Awareness, as a clear perception of the surrounding reality, appears only in those moments when circumstances throw in a little adrenaline. That is why it is so hard to do such a simple thing as waking up in a dream and saying to oneself: "Hey, guys! Stop fooling me! This is just a dream, and since it is my dream, I am the master here, and not you."

Awareness also helps you to drag intuitive information from the subconscious. This can be done, if you catch yourself thinking: "And why did I suddenly get the urge to do this?" The soul's voice is very soft and barely audible. The mind is yelling in response: "Be quiet! I know myself what I want and what I should be doing!" You need to cultivate a habit to always listen to the rustling of the morning stars. When you are half-aware of what's going on, it is practically impossible to at the right moment remember that you need to pay attention and listen to what your inner voice is saying. Even if from the very morning, you are determined to listen to the voice of your soul, you won't be able to remember it when it really matters, if you are asleep.

So, we've established that the unity of soul and mind creates external intention, while awareness gives you a chance to make external intention serve your interests. In a dream, the unity of soul and mind is attained just as easily due to the simple fact that the soul is free from the authoritarian control of the mind. In a lucid dream, there is some control, but it is directed only at adjusting the script. Everything else, even that which is beyond any common sense, is allowed. The mind agrees to accept all possible wonders in a dream. There is a scene in the fairy tale "The Tinder-box"[3] by Andersen – the princess, convinced that she is watching a dream, agrees to take a walk on the roof with the soldier. In the same way, the mind allows anything to happen, but in real life, your mind is once again desperately clinging on to its usual worldview.

It won't be that easy to reach the unity of soul and mind outside the limits of common sense. Common sense is our lifetime prison, and it won't be easy to break free. One may be keen on esoteric teachings and mysticism, be up in the clouds, believe in the incredible...But there is always room for doubt in these beliefs. The mind may pretend, but in reality, he knows that apples will fall to the ground, after all. That is why it is so difficult to completely subject external intention to one's will. Nonetheless, you may discover in your practice that awareness really does dramatically increase your chances of success.

Maximal awareness is achieved on the condition that your Watcher is always present in your mind. He provides an objective evaluation of what is going on, he keeps track of who would benefit from such a game, and he watches closely so that you wouldn't get drawn into this game like a string puppet. It is crucial that you every minute *keep in mind* the following: "are you asleep or not?" You can practice lucid dreaming, if it is not too scary. But the dream will pass, and everyday life will return. Wouldn't it be better to practice lucid living? As you see, such an alternative gives you an opportunity to organize your layer of the world just the way you like it. It is your choice to make.

Purifying Intention

External intention is an incomprehensible and huge power. And yet, you've seen how vague and elusive it can be. External intention is about control, but it is at the same time about rejecting any control. It is the will to act and a rejection of any pressure created by willpower. It is the determination to have and a rejection of striving to get something. It is all these things at the same time. To the mind, it is something new and unusual. Man is used to getting everything by only using internal intention. If you have a direct influence on the world, then it will react instantly. It is all simple and clear. But the world does not give in so easily. You have to make some effort, stand your ground, struggle and make your way through. Yet, here you are being offered a different tactic – to refuse an active attack, implying that the world itself will open its arms to you. Evidently, such a non-trivial approach will confuse your mind.

How then, should you get balance and combine the determination to have with the rejection of direct influence? The question suggests itself: you must maintain the balance of intention. That means: wanting without desiring, caring without worrying, striving without getting carried away and acting without insisting. The balance is disrupted by importance potentials. As you know, the more important the goal, the harder will be its achievement.

The expression "if you really want something, you'll definitely get it" will work very much the other way, if you are just overanxious to get something and you are making frantic attempts to get the things you want. Anxiety occurs because you are not completely convinced that your wish will be fulfilled. Compare the following two attitudes. The first one: "I really want to get what I want. It is a matter of life and death. I must get it, no matter what. I'll strain every nerve." Now, the second one: "Well, alright. I've decided that I'll get what I want. I do want it after all. So what's the problem? I'll have it, and that's that." It is not difficult to determine which position will be the winning one.

There is one more way in which a wish differs from intention – a wish does not exclude the probability of not coming true. If we wish for something and it is hard to get, then we want it even more. Desire and wishing always create excessive potentials. Desire by itself is already a potential by definition. That is when something is not present somewhere, mental energy is directed at attracting this something to that place. *Intention does not believe nor does it wish for, it simply acts.*

Pure intention would never create an excessive potential. Intention assumes that everything is already decided: "I've simply decided that this is how it will be" - it is almost an actual fact. It is you calmly realizing that this is exactly how things will be. For example, I intend to go to the newspaper stand and get a magazine. Already, there is no desire in this situation. The desire was there only until the moment when I decided to go through with it. The probability of the desire not becoming fulfilled is very slim, and should it not get fulfilled – it won't be a disaster. That is why the intention in this situation is completely free of desire, and hence, it is also free of any excessive potential.

Mental energy of desire is directed at the goal, while the energy of intention is directed at the process of attaining the goal. When a person wants something, he is creating a stir in the energy representation of the world around him. This stir brings about the action of balancing forces. But when this person is simply tramping down the street to get a newspaper, there is no longer any heterogeneity in the energy representation of the world.

This is how desire affects the representation of life tracks: I want to get it, but I am afraid I won't get it. So, I am thinking about failure (because it is important to me!) and I radiate energy on the frequency of those life tracks that include failure in their scripts. Intention acts exactly the opposite way: I know that I will get what I need. To me, this question is already settled. Thus, I radiate energy on the frequency of those tracks, where I already have what I want.

So, there are two things standing in the way of reaching a goal: desire and faith. More specifically, a great desire to reach the goal no matter what and fight whatever doubts you may have about its attainment. The more desired the goal, the more your doubts in a positive outcome will weigh. Doubt, in its turn, further raises the value of the desired. We have already clarified that desire does not help - it is simply in the way. The secret of a fulfilled wish is that *one has to say no to a desire, and replace it with intention, which is the determination to have and act.*

But the importance of your goal is in turn creating a desire to get your way no matter what and to do so by influencing the world, using internal intention. The mind, having obtained intention, rashly throws himself into war. The importance of the goal is what forces the mind to push the world in this way. In order to get just a little bit closer to external intention, one must lower importance. External intention has nothing in common with internal intention in its striving to affect the surrounding world.

External intention cannot be obtained using internal intention, no matter how strong it is. External intention is exterior to you - hence, the name. What is this thing then, after all? I have no idea. I am not afraid to admit it. It is very difficult to speak of intention within the frame of definitions that our mind is operating with.

You and I can only witness some manifestations of external intention. It appears once the soul and mind agree on something. As soon as this condition has been fulfilled, a kind of resonance is created between the radiation of mental energy and that external force, which catches us and transfers us to a corresponding sector. External intention is the force that essentially makes Transurfing happen. In other words, external intention enables the transfer along the life tracks or the movement of material realization along the sectors in the space of variations. Why does this force exist, and where does it come from? It is just as pointless to ask this question as it would be to wonder why God exists, or ponder on whether there is a link between God and external intention. Nobody knows. The important thing for us is that this force exists, and we can only be happy about the fact that we can use this force, as we would be happy because the sun is shining.

External intention indicates that it is possible for realization to move along the sectors of the space of variations. In the same way, gravity points at the possibility to fall from a roof. While you are standing on the roof, nothing is happening, despite the fact that gravity is present. But as soon as you take a step forward, that is, as soon as you yield to gravity, it grabs you and throws you down onto the ground.

In order to yield to external intention, you must reach agreement between your soul and mind. It cannot be done when importance is present. Importance gives rise to doubt and becomes an obstacle on the path to agreement. The mind desires, but the soul is resisting. The soul is striving for something, but the mind is in doubt and does not permit it. Importance throws the mind onto a closed window, while the soul is seeing an open window nearby. The soul is asking for something that she really wants with its whole heart, but importance is keeping the mind tangled in a net of common sense. Finally, unity is attained when both the soul and mind agree on what they don't want, and then external intention attempts to hand you the unwanted goods. The lack of coordination between the strivings of the soul and the mind is determined by the fact that the mind is in the power of prejudiced thoughts and false goals, forced on us by pendulums. Pendulums are once again pulling us by the very same strings of importance.

Hence, we got the second vital condition for obtaining external intention – *lowering importance and rejecting the desire to achieve a goal*. This sounds, of course, like a paradox –turns out that in order to achieve a goal, you need to abandon the desire to achieve that goal. We understand everything regarding internal intention, as we are used to acting within these limits only. We have defined intention as the determination to have and act. The difference between external intention and internal intention lies in the first and second part of this definition. *If internal intention is the determination to act, then external intention is more likely to be the determination to have.* You have a determination to trip – take a run and trip. You have a determination to find yourself on the ground – let go of yourself and yield to Earth's gravity.

The process of clearing intention from desire could be carried out according to the following formula. You are thinking about how you would reach a certain goal. Once you feel doubt – it means that you have a desire. You worry about whether you have the necessary qualities and opportunities to achieve the goal – that means that you have a desire. You believe that the goal will be achieved – even then you have a desire. You need to want and act without desiring. The intention to lift an arm and scratch your head is an example of intention that has been cleared of excessive potentials. You shouldn't have any desire, only pure intention. In order to get there, you do not have to lower internal and external importance. There is one simple and working remedy against importance: *to accept a defeat in advance.* Having not done so, you will not get rid of desire.

When clearing intention of desire, do not lose the intention itself. Intend to achieve the goal and accept your defeat in advance. Run the scenario of a possible defeat in your head a couple of times. Think about, what you will do if you fail to achieve your goal. Look for other options and insurance. After all, life won't end there, will it?

Just don't go back to the defeat scenario over and over again. It is only something you do once, and it frees you from the need to necessarily achieve the goal the way you imagined. Actually, it is beyond you to know how the goal might be achieved. We shall return to this question a bit later.

Having accepted a defeat, do not think any more about either defeat or success, but *simply keep walking towards the goal*. Move towards the goal as you would towards a newspaper stand to get a magazine. You'll find luck in your pocket, and if it is not there to be found, then you will not feel sad. If it didn't work this time, it will work the next, if you won't kill yourself over your misfortune.

To yield to external intention doesn't mean that you should abandon internal intention and sit on your hands, waiting for the agreement between your soul and mind to happen. Nothing stops you from achieving your goal by taking to common means. Rejecting desire and abandoning importance will have a positive effect on the results achieved by an active internal intention. But now you have a chance to attract a much greater force of external intention. This will enable you to achieve what seemed unachievable before.

Summary

In a conscious dream, the mind is able to control the script of the game.
Dreaming is a virtual journey of the soul in the space of variations.
Dreams cannot be interpreted as signs.
If a soul should get to a realized sector of space – it may never come back.
It is not your desire that is being realized, but rather your intention, which is the determination to have and act.
Desire is focusing attention on the actual goal.
Internal intention is focusing attention on the process of one's movement towards the goal.
External intention is focusing attention on how the goal is being realized by itself.
The goal is reached by internal intention, but it is chosen by external intention.
Internal intention strives to have a direct impact on the world.
External intention gives the green light to an independent realization of

the goal.

The laws of science only work in one single and isolated sector of space.

The work of external intention is the same as movement along the different sectors of space.

External intention is the unity of soul and mind.

The role of imagination in a dream is only to generate ideas.

The soul and mind are unanimous in negative expectations, and that is why these are easily realized.

In real life, the dream continues to a varying degree, even when you are awake.

In order to get control over external intention, you need to wake up.

As long as you are not aware of your reality, it is not under any control – it simply "happens".

It is necessary to be detached when participating in any kind of game, as if you were a performing viewer.

Awareness is attained once you are detached in the game.

Detachment implies attention and complete clarity of mind.

Awareness is not the same as controlling. Awareness is observing.

Your control must only be directed at allowing the desired script into your life.

In order to choose the right script, you need to imagine that this is how it will be.

Internal intention is the determination to act.

External intention is the determination to have.

External intention is the force that realizes Transurfing.

In order to lower the importance of your goal, you have to accept a defeat in advance.

Having accepted the defeat, do not spend any more time thinking about it, and simply walk towards your goal.

CHAPTER II

SLIDES

Why are desires not fulfilled, and dreams do not come true? In order to make the things you want your reality, you need to know how to make an "order". Starting with this chapter and onwards, you will be provided with specific practical recommendations on how to manifest your order in reality. These are the first steps of a magician.

You deserve all the very best.

Illusions

Transurfing is very careful about interpreting illusions that are the figments of imagination. There are several things people call illusions, like dreams, hallucinations, inadequate perception of reality, and finally, reality itself. If one were to leave aside inadequate perception of reality, then seeing another reality wouldn't be a product of the mind's fantasies. Dreams and hallucinations are, roughly speaking, the different journeys the soul is making in the space of variations. An illusory perception of reality is not a figment of imagination, but rather a perception of sectors, which have not been manifested in physical reality. Finally, the whole world is not an illusion. The person that dares to claim that everything perceived by him is only an illusion, is thinking too much of himself.

And why did man allow himself to claim that he is able to understand and explain everything there is? The only thing accessible to man is familiarizing with a few regularities of this world and witnessing isolated instances of its manifestations. Some manifestations of this world do not have a rational explanation. Man, on the one, hand admits to his inability to find an explanation, and declares whatever it is he has seen to be an illusion. Yet, on the other hand, he is immediately exaggerating the abilities of his mind by saying that his mind has imagined or synthesized this particular illusion.

A person under the influence of strong narcotics or alcohol is losing control of his consciousness, just as he would in a dream. Thus, the subconscious is tuning into areas in the space of variations that have not yet been realized. The body of this person is in the sector of material realization - in our material world, while his perception is wandering about in a virtual sector that is displaced relative to the realized sector. A person in a state like that may walk along familiar streets, among ordinary houses, but he would see everything in a completely different way. People and the surrounding environment do not look right. The decorations have changed. You get a reality that is half-dream and half-reality.

This is exactly how people with mental disorders perceive a different, unrealized sector, while their body is still in the sector of material realization. Their perception is tuned into a specific sector in the space of variations, where there may not only be other decorations, but another script and even different parts to play as well. Mentally ill people are not at all ill in the typical sense of illness. They do not imagine themselves to be Napoleons and other odious individuals. They are really experiencing the variation they claim to be experiencing. They see this variation in the sector of space. There are all possible variations out there, but a mentally ill person picks a variation that is more to his liking. When the conflict between his soul and mind reaches a peak and the exhausted soul is no longer able to bear the grim reality, then his perception tunes into a virtual, unrealized sector. At the same time, the person in question is physically alive in the material sector.

A psychiatrist once told a story about a woman that had a pathological desire to have an ideal husband and children. If one were to use Transurfing terminology – the importance of family was off the chart for this poor soul. As a result, she married a man that cruelly abused and taunted her. She has not been able to give birth to any children. Real life became unbearable to her, and soon enough she got into a mental institution. She no longer perceived the sector of material realization. Her body was in the material world, but her perception was tuned into a virtual sector, where she was the wife of an English lord, had children and was completely happy. From the point of view of other people, she was living in our world whilst her perception was tuned into a virtual sector.

Doctors attempt to treat such patients, but many of these patients are happy being in that particular state where illusions are much more pleasant than the cruel reality. In reality, these are no illusions at all – they are unrealized sectors, which exist and are just as real as the material sector.

Then why is the virtual sector of a mentally ill person not realized? As previously mentioned, the realization of a variation occurs when energy is modulated by a person's thoughts, in a total unity of soul and mind. Evidently, there is no unity of such kind in the case of a mental disorder. Or the displacement between the material and virtual sectors is too great, and thus requires a very large amount of energy to be realized. For example, a new Napoleon in our time would be too much of an extraordinary event, and therefore, it remains far beyond the possible flow of variations. Or perhaps there are other reasons that we do not know of to why the virtual sectors of mentally ill people are not realized.

A person is not only able to see another reality, but he is also able to experience reality in a distorted light. A person's perception relies very heavily on the information that has been imprinted on him in childhood. The following famous experiment with the two kittens could be used as an example. Two newly born kittens were placed in two separate and visually different environments. One was placed in an environment deprived of any vertical objects or lines. The other was placed in an environment where there were no horizontal objects or lines. After a period of time, the kittens were put in an ordinary room. The first kitten was constantly running against chair legs – vertical lines did not exist to him. Correspondingly, the other kitten did not have an idea about thing being horizontal and thus, he kept rolling down the stairs.

Of course, the mind is able to imagine and have fantasies, but only within the narrow limits of its previous experience. The mind is able to construct a model of a new house using old blocks.

Where is then the line between perceiving another reality and imagination? This is not a clear-cut line, but it is not that important to our goals. The only important thing here is how the inner convictions of a person influence his perception of reality and what effect it has on the life of that particular person. You are about to find out what underlies a distorted perception of reality and how much a distortion of reality may influence the actual reality.

Distortion of Reality

Man is unable to be perfectly objective when perceiving the world around him. This is similar to you putting a slide into a video projector and looking at it. Regular and even light, when passing the film, turns into a picture on the screen. So if our perception would be the screen, the light would be the world around us, and the slide would be our worldview, the representation of our understanding of the world.

Let us assume that this very moment you are worried about the way you are dressed. It may even seem to you that others are noticing you and are looking at you mockingly or with resentment. But there are no such thoughts in the minds of the people around you. These thoughts are only present in your mind, in the shape of a slide that is distorting reality. Any person is, as a rule, up to 90 percent preoccupied thinking about his own person – just like you are. Even when you are being interviewed for a job, you can be sure that the interviewer is more concerned with how to better play his part.

Slides distort your thoughts about what others think about you. *A slide is a distorted representation of reality.* A slide is something that exists in your head, but is absent in others. For example, you don't think you are attractive enough. If it doesn't really worry you, then there is no distortion. Everything is the way it is. However, it is not even about what you think about your appearance, but rather about what kind of influence the slide has on your life. If your personal appearance worries you, then you are creating the following slide in your head: "I am ugly" and you look at the world around you through that slide, as if through a filter. Such a mindset can be considered a slide because it is fixed in your thoughts only.

Physical appearance can only be judged (thus having significance attached to it) by potential partners. That is a very small percentage of the population. Others could not care less about your appearance. You don't believe me? Then ask the most respected judge - yourself: how much do you care about the appearance of other people that are not part of the potential partner pool. Most likely, you have never thought about whether a given person is attractive or not. People around you are thinking the same (or not thinking at all) about you. You can be certain that this is the case, even if you consider yourself ugly. Ugliness makes an impression only when you meet someone for the first time. After that, ugliness is no longer noticed, just as people do not pay much attention to a decoration they have become accustomed to.

So, suppose that you've put a slide concerning your unattractive appearance in your mind. You perceive everything that emanates from other people – looks, gestures, facial expressions, words - through your slide. What will you see? A friendly smile will turn into a grin. Someone's happy laughter will transform into gloating amusement at your expense. Two people are whispering to one another – they are gossiping about you. Someone briefly glanced at you – he or she gave you an angry look. Someone winced because their stomach hurt – oh god, what did he think of you? And finally, any compliment will turn into mockery. Yet, no one was actually thinking any of these thoughts. It is only in your head – it is your own slide.

Your behavior will be determined in relation to your thoughts about your unattractiveness, and it will actually make you unattractive. Your arms will start making unnatural movements, and you'll have nowhere to put them. Your face will be distorted by a tense expression, all your clever thoughts will suddenly disappear and your low self-esteem will begin its integral reign. As a result, the slide that is sitting in your imagination will be practically realized.

Slides work in two ways. On the one hand, they distort a

person's notion about his place in the world and about what others think of him. On the other hand, they distort his conception of the outside world. Everyone is particularly inclined to see the qualities of their slides in others. For example, a person does not like some inherent qualities of his character. He strives to hide them far from himself, so that he wouldn't see them. But it is impossible to conceal an unattractive slide – it sits in your head and does its thing. So, an illusion is created in that person's mind, that others think and act pretty much like he does himself. And if there are personal qualities that he does not like in himself, then he will be inclined to see the same in others. In other words, he will *project* his qualities onto other people.

Projection is when personal discontent, which has been driven into the subconscious, splashes out onto other people. The person does not want to scold himself for some of his bad sides, thus he tends to see the same bad sides in others. People are often happy to scold others for the things they do not like about themselves. And you have probably done the same thing, without being aware of it. This doesn't mean, of course, that if a person blames someone for something, then he automatically possesses the same quality. However, that does happen quite a lot. Do a little observing yourself. The position of The Watcher in role-playing will allow you to easily make out the person who is trying to direct his projection on you. If someone is wrongly blaming you, or trying to attribute qualities that are alien to you, try to ask yourself the question: perhaps the person blaming you possesses the same qualities that he is trying to project onto others? Most likely, that will be exactly the case, because if you truly do not possess any of these qualities, then the person blaming you has a slide in his head that is projecting that image.

What constitutes a slide? What film contains the slide? Importance. We return to it once again. You are worried about your looks, if it is *important* to you. The slide is in your head, but not in the heads of others, unless it is important to them. The ugliness of a person becomes an accustomed decoration to other people, because it is not of significance to them. Ugliness is only important to the person with the unusual looks. His appearance is different, and nothing more. It is the slide of importance that turns unusual appearance into ugliness.

The famous painter Henri de Toulouse-Lautrec fractured both his legs at young age, and remained a cripple all his life. While Lautrec was growing up, he was very troubled by his disfiguration. As years passed by, his physical handicap became more and more apparent, and that tormented him even more. In the end, his worrying about his imperfection reached a peak, and Lautrec was forced to accept the inevitable. He stopped caring about his disfiguration and moved on with his life. As soon as he got rid of importance, the slide ceased to exist and luck started to shine on Lautrec. He was very popular with women, not to mention that he was very successful in realizing his talent. He was, by the way, one of the founders of the famous cabaret "Moulin Rouge" in Paris, and women loved him very much. And they did so not only because of his paintings, as you understand.

Slides arise when you attach excessive value to what others think of you. If you do not know for sure what others are thinking of you, and at the same time it is very important to you, then you can be a hundred percent sure that there is a corresponding slide stuck in your head. A slide is a product of imagination, and in that sense, it could be considered an illusion. Nevertheless, such an illusion has an active effect on a person's life. This is the case when external intention is acting in a destructive way, against the will of one's mind.

A negative slide usually gives rise to unity between soul and mind. As you understand, external intention in this case is working without a hitch. It catches the owner of the negative slide and transfers him to the sector where the negative is manifested to its full potential. The transfer doesn't occur momentarily, but gradually instead. The transfer lasts throughout the entire time the slide is in the head of that person. Because of importance, he sketched a few insignificant strokes on his negative slide, and they get sharper and sharper, to finally shine in "all their glory". If a person doesn't like that he is overweight – he gains even more weight, his birthmark bothers him – it grows even larger, he feels inferior – he gets more and more evidence to support this, he is troubled with his unattractiveness – it gets worse, he is tormented by feelings of guilt – punishments come pouring down.

This continues until the person stops attributing great value to the slide or until he switches over to creating a positive slide. As soon as importance is gone, the negative slide loses its basis. It dissolves and stops working.

Should you only put in a positive, colorful slide, you will see that it works just as well as a negative one. Show yourself the positive sides of your person, and people will perceive you the same way. This is another positive quality of the slide, which could and should be used.

Positive Slides
When creating negative slides you are focusing your attention on what you do not like, what you would like to hide or get rid of. Now your task is to switch your attention to the traits you like in yourself or the traits you would like to possess. As previously demonstrated, it is not possible to hide one's flaws, but if you would want to, you could easily enhance and develop your virtues.

First, you need to do some stocktaking and uncover your negative slides. Ask yourself the question: what is it that you don't like about yourself? Which qualities in yourself would you like to hide or throw away? Slides are created unconsciously. Now, wake up and consciously look at your negative slides. In a conscious state, you'll be able to discover them easily. You need to throw this garbage out of your head. How do you do this? You can't simply get rid of them – it is not like shaving off a beard. If you were to struggle with them, they'll get even more apparent. You just need to deprive the slides of the foundation on which they stand, namely – your attention and the value that you attach to them. You need to switch your attention from the negative to the positive. Never mind everything that troubled you before, and stop fighting yourself. Turn away from all your flaws and switch your attention to your virtues instead, the ones you have and the ones you would like to have.

Is it *important* to you to hide your flaws? That is the basis for a negative slide. Is it *important* to you that you make a good impression? That will be the basis for a positive slide. Everything remains in its place; the only thing that has changed is the direction of your attention, your importance.

Draw yourself, as you want to see yourself. It won't be a self-deception, because it would be a conscious game. You were deceiving yourself, when you were fighting your flaws, thinking that you could hide or destroy them with your inner intention. Create a slide for yourself where you shine with all your glory. Love yourself in that slide and nurture it, adding more and more details to the slide.

A slide doesn't have to contain a static image. This might be a perception of you moving with grace and confidence, how elegantly you are dressed, which aristocratic manners you possess, how you shine with your intellect, radiating charm, how you win other people's favor, how easily you manage problems and so on. Now put the slide in your head – and go ahead! A positive slide, just like a negative one, will have a direct influence on your actions and behavior. Unwillingly and even unconsciously, you will adjust to the slide. But the main workload will be done by external intention in accordance with image on the slide.

Keep reproducing the created image in your thoughts until the slide dissolves. What does that mean? As time passes by, the slide will practically become a part of you, and at that point, it will no longer be a slide. When you get the desired, it will no longer be of importance to you. Importance will disappear, and the slide will dissolve, yet its mission would have been completed. That would mean that your soul has agreed with your mind. That will definitely happen. After all, you want it with both your soul and mind. While the mind is trying to turn the slide into reality, deep down in your soul, you are still aware of the fact that this is nothing but a game in disguise. But if you will keep fixating the image of the slide methodically and systematically, the soul will get used to it and she will eventually agree to consider the slide as an integral part of herself. Keep in mind that external intention is unable to instantly realize the slide – it does so gradually.

As you see, it is not that hard to get the desired results. It is all about the determination to have. Slide images could belong to any traits or qualities, which you believe you lack. However, you must be aware of how realistic it is to manifest the particular slide in the real world. Don't draw the ideal picture right away. It is better to start with something you could actually attain. With time, you will be able to move up to a higher level.

Under no circumstances should you copy an image from people who you think possess the necessary qualities! Your slide must be yours and yours only, and not a copy of a stranger. We will discuss this more thoroughly in the next chapter. But for now, let's just note that any quality has a replacement that at the given stage will fit you more. Courage could be replaced with determination, beauty – with charm, strength – with dexterity, being a skilled speaker – with ability to listen, intellectuality – with consciousness, physical perfection – with confidence. Having set realistic, attainable goals, you are giving external intention a chance to complete your mini-orders faster and get to work, realizing more difficult tasks.

Positive slides are particularly effective and fast working, when you are about to meet new people, who do not yet have any idea of who you are. This could be an interview, a contest, a party or something like that. Go ahead and put the wanted slide in your head, and don't worry about a thing. Don't forget about the image on the slide – keep it in your consciousness at all times. Allow yourself the luxury of getting rid of all hesitations and doubts like "what if it won't work out". After all, having thrown away all your doubts, you have nothing to lose. If your determination to have will be enough, you will achieve maximum and sometimes even the most incredible success.

Positive slides could be made not only in regards to your persona, but also in regards to the world around you. Such slides will let everything positive through and will keep the negative out. If you remember, we have already discussed the topic of *trans-*

mitting positive energy in the chapter "The Wave of Success". No matter how you slice it pays, first of all, to be open to everything that is positive, and to ignore everything that is negative. You stop by the exhibits you fancy and indifferently walk by the ones that you do not like. In this regard, the world differs from an exhibition in that *the negative will pursue you, if you won't pass it by indifferently.* The positive, in turn, will always be with you, if you are happy to accept it.

It may seem that positive slides are a bit like rose-colored glasses. Despite the general opinion, the notion of rose-colored glasses was invented by pessimists and not by optimists. Pessimists are pragmatically afraid of seeing everything in rose color and didactically warn the optimists of the danger it may entail. Such pragmatism is nothing other than a negative slide. A pessimist does not dare to allow himself the luxury of having, and so he receives accordingly.

You shouldn't worry too much about the fact that a positive slide also distorts reality. In most cases, such distortion is insignificant, as inner control nonetheless does its part. Distortion, provoked by a positive slide, will only do well, unless, of course, you will imagine yourself to be Napoleon. It is good to do everything in moderation and to keep the excessive potentials in mind. With their distortion, negative slides have an immeasurably more harmful effect on one's life. But distortion is still not the major thing. The main quality of the slides is that external intention slowly but safely manifests them in reality.

Expanding your Comfort Zones

Let's say you have an ambitious desire to become a star or a millionaire. Yet, are you ready to let yourself have it? People usually think that fame, money or power is the lot of the chosen ones. But who picks these chosen ones? First of all – the chosen ones pick themselves, and only then are they picked by all the other people. If you dream of something but you are not ready to let yourself have it – you won't get it.

A homeless person is standing on the street; he is looking

through a window, at a Christmas table in someone else's house. Is he ready to let himself sit at that table and have a meal? Sure, if he'll get invited, he'll do it. To enter a house and to sit at the table is the readiness to act, that is – internal intention. But who would invite him? And he understands that perfectly well. The Christmas table is the layer of the world that belongs to someone else. Is he ready to have this table at his house, in the layer of his world? No, the homeless knows that he doesn't have a house nor does he have any money or a way to earn it. External intention won't give him anything, because while he is within the boundaries of common sense, he is not ready to *have*.

Let's assume that you want to be a wealthy man or woman. But are you ready to receive such a gift from destiny? Of course, if someone were to give away a "spare" million, any of us would take it without hesitating. And wealth would not destroy your life, as some people try to show in edifying films. But I am not talking about that. Are you ready to *take* that million? You probably thought that I am talking about that one must earn the million, didn't you? Again, that is not it. Are you ready to simply make a choice? *To let yourself have?*

You need to get used to the thought that you will achieve your goal. If you want to become a wealthy person, but you are afraid of entering expensive shops at the same time, then nothing will happen. If you experience even the slightest discomfort in an expensive shop, then you are not ready to let yourself have expensive things. The people working in stores like that can instantly identify whether the person that entered their shop is a potential buyer or he or she is just a curious fellow with an empty wallet. A buyer behaves as if he owned the place. He is calm, confident and dignified – he is aware of his right to choose. The curious and very zealous, but poor person behaves as an uninvited guest. He acts in a constrained, tense and timid manner. He feels the measuring eyes of the shop assistants and he is almost apologizing for entering such a prestigious establishment. He is creating a whole bunch of excessive potentials at the same time: craving, envy, feelings of being inadequate, irritation and dissatisfaction.

All of this happens because not only is he not ready to let himself have it financially, but he doesn't even *consider himself worthy* of having expensive things. After all, your soul understands everything the mind is telling her literally, and the mind is saying the same thing over and over again: "All these things are not for us. We are poor people, and so we have to do with something more modest".

Let yourself be worthy of all this luxury. You are really worthy of all the best. For the only purpose to keep you under control, destructive pendulums made you believe that everyone should know their place. Be bold - go to the expensive shops and look at the items on display like a master, and not like a servant in a wealthy house. It is, of course, pointless to practice autosuggestion, trying to convince yourself that you can afford to buy an item in an expensive shop. You won't be able to fool yourself, and it is not even necessary. How to believe it and let yourself have it?

First of all, let's draw a line between the areas of internal and external intention in the phrase "being ready to let yourself have something". A person that is used to thinking and acting within the boundaries of common sense tends to cut to the chase: "I just can't afford it, period. What else could be said about that?" And you don't have to try to convince yourself that you can buy an expensive item, when there is an empty wallet in your pocket. That is really not the point. Internal intention implies a determination to act that is the determination to get some money. But since there is nowhere to get the money from, your mind passes a pragmatic verdict. When you are acting within the limits of internal intention, you won't achieve anything for sure. External intention won't just fall on your head like heavenly manna. Where would it come from, when you are not ready to let yourself have? External intention implies the determination to have, in other words, to consider yourself worthy and to *know* that you are the one making the choice. Not to believe or to think that you are worthy, but to know it for a fact.

Deep down in your soul you are always having some doubts about that your wishes will come true nonetheless. *Even if you are ready to act to fulfill your desire – it won't be enough.* When you don't believe, then you are not letting yourself feel that you are worthy, or you simply doubt that your desire can be fulfilled. Now, those people that became stars and millionaires are not different from you in any skills or qualities, but they are different in that they allowed themselves to have what they wanted. *You need to let yourself have.* This state could be likened to the feeling you had when you were able to ride a bicycle for the first time. Doubts, hesitations and arguments disappeared; the only thing remaining was silent clarity – knowledge. *The feeling of clarity without words, knowing something without believing, confidence without hesitation is the state of unity between the soul and mind.* When you are in a state like that, you feel like an integral part of the unspoken force that rules the Universe. That force grabs you and transfers you to the sector, where the things your soul and mind agreed upon come true.

Everyone is free to choose whatever he or she likes, but far from everybody believes that they are given free hands. No matter what I tell you, you still do not completely believe that the freedom of choice is real, do you? Our life confirms the opposite, because all people are under the influence of pendulums. But even if you have freed yourself from the influence of pendulums, the freedom of choice is still beyond your comfort zone. It is too unreal – to have the right to choose in the world of pendulums. It's too incredible. In your heart, you don't believe that having a dream that is hard to achieve is only a matter of personal choice. But *positive slides will help you to introduce the incredible into your comfort zone.* Once you stop feeling inner discomfort because of the idea that any dream is accessible, your hesitations will fade, and your belief will turn into knowledge. Your soul will come to an agreement with your mind, and that is when you will have the determination to have.

Trying to convince your soul of something is pointless. After all, she doesn't reason, she knows. A soul can only be trained. She must get accustomed to the new comfort zone. That's why you need slides. With the help of the slides, the unity between the soul and mind is achieved gradually. This fortress can only be taken by a prolonged siege. Create the slide of your dream in your head and keep it in your consciousness at all times. Return to the drawn image again and again. Work on the details, draw new features of the image of your dream.

Don't look at the slide as an outside observer, immerse yourself in it and live in it, at least virtually. Every time you try to picture the slide as a film on the screen, remind yourself that doing so has little effect on achieving the goal. You must play the scenes in your mind, feeling like an active participant in these scenes, and not like a viewer at the cinema. No matter what you do, always play the slide in your thoughts. You can think about something else, but the image of the slide must be the background. Playing the slide must turn into a habit. *A slide will only give results, if it has been played systematically and for a long time.*

Be actively interested in everything that has anything to do with the topic of your dream. *Let in all of the necessary information. Give it a chance to enter the layer of your world.* It's great, if you have the possibility to play the slide in real life, even if only formally. For example, you could practice choosing in those expensive shops we talked about. Don't think about the money and don't look at the prices. Your goal is not the money, but what could be bought for it. It is enough to be around it, to feel the taste, to choose, to simply and calmly look at things and evaluate them. Let all these things into you. Don't look at them as if they were some unattainable luxury, but rather as if they were something you are about to buy. Pretend to be the master of these things. Let the shop assistants think that you are a buyer. Play the game of a thorough buyer (as long as it is not the game of an arrogant buyer). By letting these things into yourself, you are tuning into those life tracks where these things will be yours.

You don't have to worry about how these things will become yours. If you have the determination to have, external intention will find a way that you wouldn't even think of. Just don't be thinking later that it was an accident, a coincidence or some mysterious occurrence. I don't recall who said the following: "Chance is the pseudonym of God, when He doesn't want to sign"[4].

If you experience even the most fleeting feelings of awe before the world of your dreams, make them go away. It is your world, and there is nothing unattainable for you in your world. External or internal importance will be an obstacle on your way to unity between soul and mind. The world of your dreams must be a happy place, but at the same time, it must be an ordinary place, in the sense that if you have something, then to you it is in the order of things, it is normal. In order to tune into the corresponding life tracks, you must feel as if you already have what you want. It is not self-deception, because you are playing this game in a conscious state.

The determination to have can be best demonstrated by using the example of the newly fledged Russian billionaires that are greater in number than the billionaires of the developed countries. In the end of 1980's, during the period of Perestroika in Russia, the dull-witted politicians thought that socialist economy would instantly turn into market economy, if everything were to be privatized. Those, who happened to be at the feeding rack at the right time and got the picture, got rich immediately, and without any greater effort. Everything that belonged to the government during the socialist period, namely - oil, gas, gold, diamonds and all other natural, industrial and intellectual resources now belonged to a handful of oligarchs. What belonged to everyone was now property of some oligarch. He didn't have to do business like the real billionaires did, which had to work for their millions. Those that were the closest to the feeding rack only had to put their hands on and growl: "Mine" – and then formalize it as a legal act.

For what reasons did the things that belonged to everyone now became the property of some oligarch? This period is, of course, unique in the history of Russia. But there were plenty of intelligent and talented people, who were standing close to the riches of Russia, and yet most of them were left empty handed. Those, who allowed themselves to have, were able to grab what was lying in front of them. The new rich had no feelings of guilt, remorse, doubts or inferiority. They didn't consider themselves to be unworthy, and it didn't occur to them to feel guilty in expensive shops. They had the determination to have, and that is why the passionless external intention gave them what they wanted. That is the way it is. And you are telling me that things like that are inconceivable!

Visualizing the Goal

The ways of achieving goals in Transurfing are outside the boundaries of common sense and standard ideas. The method of achieving a goal that is the closest to the practice of Transurfing - is goal visualization. You basically imagine the desired with as much detail as possible and then keep that image in your head at all times.

The common worldview considers visualization as a waste of time. Indeed, he that walks will overcome the road, and not the one who is daydreaming. But, regardless of how things are, a mental representation of the goal is of the same critical importance as the actual process of attaining the goal, and you already know why that is the case. The one who is simply "walking" will achieve average results and will live just like the rest, contributing his share to the triumph of common sense. The pilgrim that has the methods of Transurfing in his bag will achieve results that common sense is trying to fit into such notions as "luck", "coincidence" or "fortune's chosen".

Everything is upside down in Transurfing, if you look at it from the common sense's point of view. Although, one could say the same about common sense from the position of Transurfing. If you do not wish to live like everybody else, if you do not want to be content with average results, if you strive to get everything in your life "full scale", then you are a *Wanderer*. A wanderer of Transurfing is not chosen by destiny – instead, destiny is his chosen one. You will achieve everything you want, if you will manage to shake the monolith of your common sense. Now, it does not mean in any way that you should fly up to the clouds. It means the opposite – to come back down to earth, because common sense is the one up in the clouds. You have seen this more than once and soon you will discover more remarkable things.

We will have to figure out why visualizing a set goal does not always yield results. Even the active followers of the esoteric and of non-traditional psychology cannot rely on it to a hundred percent. There are simple and rather difficult visualization methods. They have a varied success rate. Some things work out, and some – don't. I am personally not satisfied with such a quality, and you would probably not be either. Therefore, I would like to reassure you: visualization in Transurfing is something very different from what is usually understood by that word. Transurfing visualization is actually working to a hundred percent.

The known types of visualization can be put into three groups. The first group – dreams. From a practical point of view, this is the weakest and the least reliable kind of visualization. It won't harm you to dream, but it is practically useless. *Dreams do not come true!* Daydreamers do not usually lay any serious claim to the manifestation of their dreams. It only seems to them that they would really want their dreams to come true. But deep down inside they either don't believe that their dream could come true, or they have no intention to have or act. Daydreamers view their dreams as distant as the stars. When somebody hints to them about castles in the sky, they close their shells, like oysters: "Don't touch my dream!" If one were to give a specific definition to the goal of dreamers, then it would be nothing more than the actual process of dreaming.

The second group is film. I don't mean cinematography, but rather a film about your desires in your thoughts. Playing the film in one's head is an intentional process, and that is the only thing different from simply dreaming of something. There is the intention to have and act, and one of the actions is visualizing the manifested desire by looking at the film. How does it happen? For example, you want to have a house and you picture it this way and that, in every detail - according to the rules. You have a completely clear or an almost clear picture in your head of what the house would look like, and you carry that image in your head throughout the day.

Let's suppose that you've completed the task brilliantly. One would think that your wish would come true. Guess what you will get? Well, you will definitely see that house – almost or exactly the way you pictured it. But it won't be yours. It will be somebody else's house on the street or in a movie. Because you get what you order. After all, you've made such an honest effort visualizing the house, but you haven't in any way explained to the "waiter" that the house is yours. Thus, he accurately carried out your order. You were so caught up with the quality of the visualization process, just as it was described to you in books that you forgot about the most important thing – who should be the owner of the house. That is the main mistake of those practicing this kind of visualization. A movie will remain a movie. You will never be part of it. *Why, you are gaping at it, like a beggar gaping at the shop windows!*

The third group of visualization – you are not watching a film like a viewer, but you are taking part in it in your thoughts. This is already much more effective. When you are playing your character, you are setting the parameters of your radiation onto corresponding life tracks. For example, your goal is to have a new house. Do not look at it in your thoughts, as if it was a picture. Create a kind of virtual dream for yourself when you are awake. Enter the house, walk around in it, go into the different rooms, and touch all the things around you. Lounge in the armchair that's opposite to the fireplace, feel the cosy warmth and the smell of smoke, put some more firewood into the fireplace. Go into the kitchen and look into the refrigerator. What's in there? Go to sleep in a comfortable bed. Are you comfortable? Sit at the table with your family. Have a housewarming party. Move some furniture. Touch the grass in the garden with your bare hands. The grass is green and soft. Plant some flowers. What flowers do you like? Pick an apple off the apple tree and eat it. Feel yourself at home. It is your home, after all. Do not look at it with the eyes of a suffering dreamer, with awe, as if it was something unattainable or some remote possibility. You already have this house. Pretend that it is for real.

As you understand, this visualization represents a slide. Such a slide will expand your comfort zone and it will definitely manifest itself with time. But nobody knows when it will happen. Perhaps you will have to wait for a long time. It all depends on how you work with this slide. If you have played with it a little and then dropped it, you shouldn't be expecting any results. There are no miracles in real life.

When you are working with a slide, you must keep in mind the following. First, if you've grown cold towards your goal, the slide will dissolve, and you will have to force yourself to work with it, which you will very soon grow tired of. Then you need to think - do you really need that slide? Second, you must keep in mind that external intention does not immediately realize a slide; it gradually takes you to the life tracks of your goal. You will need to stay calm, have patience and be persistent.

Persistence is only needed at the first stage of the process. Later, visualizing the slide will turn into a habit and you will no longer have to force yourself. Well, and finally, if the goal is not yours, but was forced on you by pendulums, you won't reach any agreement between your soul and mind. I will talk about that in the upcoming chapters. But if you are striving towards the goal with all your heart, then visualizing the slide will definitely get results. Once you will have the true determination to have, external intention will find a way to realize your goal.

If you thought that a slide is the method of visualization in Transurfing – you were wrong. Even a slide of the highest quality can take a long time to realize, especially if the goal is in a rather distant sector of the space of variations. The process of achieving a goal can be accelerated with the help of Transurfing visualization. You are about to find out what it is.

Visualizing the Process

Let's do the following little problem. Let's say your end goal is to get rich. To achieve the goal, you are visualizing a case full of money. The visualization is carried out by all the rules of the third group and for a sufficient period of time. Question: what will come of this and when?

Answer: nothing will ever happen. You could do this everyday for the rest of your life, and still, in the best-case scenario, you would simply see cases with money more often – in films. The probability of you finding a treasure or winning the lottery is very small. Should you bet on the probability?

You could ask the question: how could this be? After all, I constantly picture in my mind how I open the case with my hands, get my money, stroke it, and almost lick it! The visualization of the third group is not a movie, what else do I have to do? And what about the almighty external intention?

If one were examine the situation from the point of view of Transurfing, then one would identify two mistakes. First – a briefcase full of money is not your goal. Money is only an attribute. It is not even a means of reaching a goal, not to mention being a goal itself. However, we shall discuss your goals later, so let's not rush ahead. The second mistake is – *focusing on the final goal. Unless you are only one step away, focusing on the final goal is not moving you towards your goal in any way.* Your comfort zone is, of course, expanding, and external intention is doing what it should. But *you are not helping it in any way.* You have to at least move your legs! I'm not talking about the fact that you also need to act. Now we are only discussing the process of visualization.

Until now, your common experience has advised you that if you want to get something, you need to turn all your thoughts and ambitions towards your goal. You will have to forget about that. Just as I've promised you, Transurfing works unconditionally, but you need to abandon some common ideas and to accept other incredible ones, considered as such from a normal point of view.

Let's define the main and the most basic difference between visualization in Transurfing and the usual visualization process. As you know, focusing on the goal – is desire. Focusing on the movement towards the goal – is intention. The driving force behind any action is intention, and not desire. Thus, it is not you contemplating the goal that is moving you forward towards the goal, but rather you *visualizing the process of approaching the goal.* The realization of intention – is a process, and not focusing on one shot. Of course, the goal itself is also part of the visualized image.

However, the focus lies on *the process of approaching* the goal, while the goal is only in the background of you moving towards it.

Visualizing the actual goal differs from visualizing the process of achieving the goal in much the same way as desire differs from intention. Desire doesn't do anything. Let's again return to the example with lifting the arm. Imagine that you wish to lift your arm. First, think about that you want to lift your arm, and about the result – that is your lifted arm. And now – lift it up. In the first case, your desire is working and nothing is being done. Basically, what's happening is that you are only stating the fact that you have a desire to lift an arm, and you are visualizing the goal – your lifted arm. In the second case, intention is at work, and it works the whole time while the arm is being lifted. During this process, it is implied that the goal is something you need to strive for but you are focusing on the actual process of reaching the goal. Ultimately, in order to get somewhere, it is not enough to simply wish for it and picture yourself where you want to be. You must take steps. That is, you need to carry out the process.

It could seem that all of this is just trivial reasoning. Yet, look what conclusion we arrive at y using this argument: *visualizing the goal is the work of desire, and thus the goal is not getting any closer.* Turns out you're shooting blanks by simply wishing for something to happen.

In Transurfing, you *visualize the process of approaching the goal –* intention is working in this case, thus the goal will be achieved sooner or later. Moving towards the goal is not something that happens as fast as it does in dreams, but the movement is there, and it is quite tangible! Having studied the last chapter, you will even be able to actually *see your movement along the various life tracks.*

No matter what you are doing, if it is a lengthy process, visualizing that process will be helpful. Such visualization is especially useful when doing something creative, when the final goal is not clear-cut. What do we understand by visualizing the process? Let say, you are working on some art object, and you don't yet really know what it will look like, once you are finished. Nonetheless, you know about the properties that you would like this object to possess. In between your work sessions, try to imagine how the object is getting more and more perfect. Today you've completed a few details of your work of art. And tomorrow you intend to add new strokes. Imagine how your creation is transforming more and more. You are giving it more and more properties, and it turns into a masterpiece right in front of your eyes. You are pleased, caught by the creative process, and your baby is growing with you.

You won't have a problem coming up with a visualization method that is appropriate for your situation. The secret is not only to contemplate your object, but also to picture the process of the birth and growth of perfection. You do not have to imagine how your creation, for example, a work of art is being drawn, modeled, built on its own. You are the one creating it. It is being perfected in your hands. *You are creating and admiring your work at the same time.*

A good example would be a mother caring for her child, bringing him up. She feeds him, puts him to bed and imagines her baby growing every day. She cares for him, considers him lovely and confirms to herself that he is getting cuter and cuter. The mother is playing with him, teaching him and, at the same time, she is imagining her baby boy getting smarter, and that he will soon go to school. As you see, this is not about contemplating the process; instead, it is about creation and simultaneous visualization of the process. The mother is not simply observing her child growing up, but she is also picturing his development and the kind of a person he is growing up to be.

If computer software is your creation then, when you go home after work, imagine how it is getting even more efficient and convenient. Tomorrow you will add more details, and your software will surprise everyone.

If you are working on a business-project, then imagine how more and more brilliant ideas are popping up in your head. Every day you put forward new and original suggestions. Watch your project developing and keep telling yourself that it is turning into an example of professionalism.

If you are working with your body, then raise it like a mother would a child. Imagine your body gradually getting the desired shape. Nurture it, train it and then picture your body growing muscles in some places, and tightening in others.

In any case, visualize the process: the way your work is moving towards completion. *Simple contemplation of the end result expands the comfort zone, and that is already something. But while visualizing the process of approaching the goal, you are significantly accelerating the work of external intention.*

If you do not know yet how your goal might be realized – don't worry. Keep visualizing the slide calmly and systematically. Once the goal is completely integrated within you comfort zone, then external intention will throw in a suitable option. Don't toss about, desperately trying to find ways of achieving your goal. Throw importance aside and rely on the flow of variations. Don't be looking at the slide – live it. Then you'll involuntarily be going in the right direction.

But visualizing the process is not all there is to it. The material realization of the space of variation is inert, like tar. Hence, the transfer must be done gradually, unless, of course, you have the external intention of a messiah. Gradually does not only mean that it is a continuous process, the transfer should also be done in stages. That is the secret behind another property of the Transurfing visualization process.

Transfer Chains
If the goal is located on sufficiently distant life tracks, then it is practically impossible to set your radiation onto those tracks. For example, if you are about to sit an exam, but you do not know anything about the subject, you won't be able to tune into the track, where you successfully pass the exam. Visualizing yourself answering a question correctly won't work, if you do not know anything at all.

There could be a relatively long way (not necessarily measured in time) between your future goal and your present situation. Not only will your situation change, but so will your way of thinking and acting, and perhaps, even your personality will change. You won't be able to set all your parameters right without having done that journey.

If you were to try to practice visualizing the process of moving towards a rather distant goal, you would be tempted to rush ahead and try to make everything happen faster. That will take you nowhere. As a result, you'll feel disappointed and annoyed, which will in turn set the balancing forces against you.

You could play the images of a distant future in your head as much as you'd like, and nothing bad will happen. Yet, *visualizing a process of moving along a track that you will not enter soon, may bring you to God knows where.* Imagine that you have to go down a meandering river. You wouldn't be dragging your boat along the bank as a shortcut, in order to skip the river bends, would you?

If the goal has to be attained through several stages, then you will have to go through each stage in order, whether you want it or not. For example, you cannot become a professional in any area in one go. You must first finish an educational institution, then find a job, then work on perfecting your professionalism and so on. Such a stage-by-stage path in the space of variation is called a *transfer chain.* Each chain link – is a separate stage. The stages are linked together, and this is because if you haven't passed a particular stage, then you won't be able to enter the stage that comes after that. For example, you cannot enter a graduate program, if you haven't got an undergraduate degree.

A separate link on the transfer chain is put together from interconnected and relatively homogenous sectors of space. The way to the goal is structured and made out of transfer chains and the flow of variation. The space of variations has a well-ordered structure. If you are pursuing your goal in an unorganized manner then you will never reach it. You already know what to do to avoid falling out of the flow of variations – do not create excessive potentials, don't beat the water with your hands and do not fight the current. Only one rule remains to follow: apply visualization (where you picture the process of moving towards the goal) to your current stage only. You are welcome to imagine the end result as much as you want, as long as it is in the form of a slide. But you should only picture the process of moving towards the goal within the limits of the current link in a transfer chain. Don't rush – you'll get everything done in due time.

Now I am able to provide the final definition of visualization in Transurfing. *Visualization in Transurfing – is a mental image of the process that realizes the current link on the transfer chain.* By a mental image of the process, I mean getting your thoughts in the right direction. You just need to give your thoughts a push, and they'll proceed on their own, just like in a script in your dream. You must live by the process that realizes the link in your thoughts, as well as in your actions. Your thoughts and your actions must be coordinated.

As you can see, it is simple. It is not hard to find out what the separate links are in your own transfer chain. And what if you do not know the order of progress? Or you have no idea by what means and which path may lead you to your goal? It is no big deal, so don't let it worry you. I once again repeat what you should do in cases like that.

If you do not know yet how your goal might be realized – don't worry. Keep visualizing the slide calmly and systematically. Once the goal is completely integrated within your comfort zone, the external intention will throw in a suitable option. Don't toss about, desperately trying to find ways of achieving your goal. The slide will make you act in the right direction involuntarily and even unconsciously. Throw importance aside, stay calm and rely on the flow of variations.

Here, I would like to add a few words about signs. If you are interpreting a sign that you believe could point at the possibility of reaching the goal, then you must know that these signs can only be applied to the current link on the transfer chain. They have only a distant relation to the end goal. In other words, the indicators are only related to the path you are walking on now. You may interpret the signs for all those questions that concern the current link on the transfer chain. But if the current track of your life is separated several links away from the goal, then the signs cannot serve as goal indicators. That does not mean that there are no signs for the distant goal at all. It is just that you cannot interpret them with a significant degree of reliability. On the whole, interpreting signs, apart from emotional comfort of your soul, is the least reliable method in Transurfing. Thus, you shouldn't attach great importance to signs and their interpretation.

Now, we only have to establish what role the third group visualization is playing in all of this, and whether one should be visualizing the goal at all. The answer is simple: definitely. It is absolutely crucial that you are practicing visualization in any way that is convenient for you. The goal is maintained in your head in the form of a slide, which expands the comfort zone and sets the frequency of mental radiation on the life tracks associated with the goal. This is the main and only function of the third group visualization. However, the actual transfer to the life tracks that are associated with the goal is still being done by the little working horse of Transurfing – the visualization of the process of moving towards the goal. By visualizing the process, you are uniting your inner intention with external intention.

Summary

Illusions – is not a product of your imagination. It is a vision of another reality.

Any man living in the material world is able to perceive an alternative reality.

Your perception of the world could be distorted by your own inner presumptions.

A slide is something that exists in your mind, but not in the minds of others.

Slides distort reality.

Man tends to project his slides onto others.

Importance is the basis of a slide.

Once importance has gone, the slide ceases to exist.

Stop fighting yourself and switch your attention from the negative to the positive.

Create a positive slide for yourself that is pleasant for both mind and soul.

Examine your slide more often, and keep adding more details.

Under no circumstances should you copy the appearance of a slide from other people.

If you do not have the determination to have, you will not get what you want.

Allow yourself the luxury of being worthy of all the best there is.

The determination to have is knowing for sure that you are worthy and that the choice is yours.

Positive slides will help you to introduce the incredible into your comfort zone.

Do not look at the slide, as if it were a picture. Live in it, at least virtually. Take in any information that is from the world of your dreams.

Simply contemplating the result will not get you to your goal; visualizing the process of moving towards your goal will.

Do not contemplate the result. Instead, imagine a process of creation and growth of perfection.

Visualization in Transurfing is a mental image of the realization process that the current link of a transfer chain is undergoing.

If do not yet know how to reach your goal, keep visualizing the slide. The slide itself will get you in the right direction.

CHAPTER III

YOUR SOUL AND YOUR MIND

Man possesses great power, which is sometimes referred to as psychic energy. Everyone has magic abilities, but they are deeply buried within. Apparently, you do not have to go to great lengths to unlock your inner reserves and potential. The wondrous is just around the corner, but man doesn't notice it.

The soul enters this world, just like a child, trustingly extending her little arms.

The Wind of Intention

Man is born an individual – a unique being. This individuality of his is later developed. Thoughts, knowledge, convictions, habits and even his personality emerge later, like a thin coating. And yet, all of this didn't simply appear on an empty space. What was there, in the beginning? If it was just a blank sheet of paper, then try to be a blank paper for a minute. Close your eyes and stop any thoughts going through your mind. If one were to contemplate black emptiness, then for a few moments one would manage not to have a single thought in one's head. Say, in a given moment, there are no longer any thoughts in your head – you've reached a state of emptiness. But have you stopped being you in that moment? Your mind's activity has been paused, but some kind of integral feeling that you are you remains.

And how would you explain that you - are you? Usually, a man becomes aware of himself as an individual in the context of his social position. But imagine for a second the social environment is gone and you find yourself "suspended" in space. You have nothing: no society, no Earth, no Sun, no past, no future – there is nothing but a black void around you. Everything is gone, there is only you left. And what remains of you and your former persona? All your knowledge and thoughts had to do with your living environment. Your habits, manners, desires, fears, interests, personality – too were only operating in association with that living environment. But it is gone now. What is then left of you?

It is very difficult to discuss this question within the framework of our mind's conceptions. In this book, we won't be addressing the ancient issue of whether the soul exists or not. It would take a lot of time and it wouldn't get use anywhere. The question is of no principal significance to the aims of Transurfing. If you would like to – then do believe in the soul's existence, or maybe in the existence of the subconscious. You could agree with the conception of immortality – or not. There is only one thing that is beyond any doubt – the human psyche includes the conscious as well as the unconscious.

From the very beginning we agreed that we would relate all that is conscious to the mind, and all that is unconscious – to the soul. For simplicity and practical benefit, we would only need to clarify a very small and narrow part of the soul issue. It's enough to only draw a rough line between the soul and the mind: feelings are for the soul, and thoughts are for the mind. Experiencing a feeling of delight and inspiration, or like you have got wings – those are the feelings of the soul. Feeling heavy-hearted and depressed are also states experienced by the soul.

The mind is completely in the grip of pendulums and his own ideas and preconceptions, which in turn have been forced on him by the very same pendulums. The level of a person's freedom is limited by the narrow boundaries of what is allowed. That person is mistakenly taking his role in this world to be that of either a servant or a master. From Transurfing's point of view neither of these positions is correct. Man is nothing. He is only a drop that, for a moment, flew up from the ocean.

One could use the splashes of the sea waves to illustrate the process of birth and death. A drop that has been separated from the ocean cannot feel as one with the ocean and get energy from it. That separated drop believes that it exists on its own and has nothing to do with the ocean. But once the drop falls back into the ocean, it will become aware of being as one with the ocean. The drop and the ocean merge into one. Their essence is one and the same – it is water.

A separate water particle could take on different forms: a drop, a snowflake, a piece of ice, a steam cloud. The forms are different but their substance is the same. A water particle doesn't recall or understand that it is the same with the ocean. The particle thinks that the ocean is – waves, foam, splashes, icebergs, calm water...In the same way, the particle is thinking that it is a drop, or a snowflake, or a little steam cloud. It is hard for the particle to make out the one common substance that is behind its numerous external forms, namely water. It is something familiar, but yet unclear and subtle.

The biblical texts, concerning this issue, reveal the truth that has been distorted by the mind's conceptions. The claim that God made man in his own image is true. It is only that it is often being understood the wrong way. God could assume any form, but His substance is not that He has a head, two arms and two legs. If one were to liken God to an ocean, and man to a drop, then they have one common substance – water.

According to people that have been on the border between life and death, the soul experiences an inexplicable calm and bliss when feeling that she is as one with the Cosmos. The drop returned to the ocean, and it once again became aware of its former nature: the drop is of the same essence as the ocean. All of the ocean's energy is moving through the drop.

Throughout the entire history of humankind and human civilization, people have been striving to summon the feeling of being as one with the Cosmos, while being still alive. All schools of spiritual development are in the end pursuing the same goal: to attain enlightenment or, in other words, to feel as one with this world, to dissolve in the ocean of energy, and at the same time not to lose oneself as an individual being.

What does a man get, having reached enlightenment? The entire energy of the ocean – the Universe – is at his disposal. He doesn't see any substantial difference between himself and this infinity. His mental energy gets into resonance with the energy of the ocean. This is the moment when *the intention of the enlightened one turns into external intention* – this great and incredible force that rules the world.

When the shape of a kite satisfies the necessary parameters, it soars up by the air streams. In the same way, a man is caught and carried by the wind of external intention, and flies away to the sector of space that corresponds to the parameters of his mental radiation. For purposeful movement in the space of variations, he has to sense this wind of external intention just as clearly, as if he were to sense the movement of air or water.

Until a man realizes the essence and nature of his sameness with the ocean, he won't be able to control external intention. We won't make enlightenment our goal. It is too difficult of a task. However, you do not need to reach enlightenment to realize your goals. There is no need to retire to Tibet and practice meditation. Transurfing offers a loophole that allows you to get some control over external intention, only a little bit, but it will be enough to make your dreams come true.

The principle behind this loophole is simple enough. Mind has the will, but it is unable to control external intention. The soul is able to be as one with external intention, but has no will of its own. It is flying in the space of variations, as an uncontrollable kite. *In order to submit external intention to your will, you only have to obtain the unity of your soul and mind.*

This is a rather hard but yet an accomplishable feat. As it has already been demonstrated, the work of external intention is quite evident in the realization of our worst fears. In this case, external intention is working against the will of our mind. Now we only have to determine, what one should do in order to realize one's best expectations. In the chapter called "Intention", we have already identified the primary conditions that need to be fulfilled in order to master external intention: *awareness, lowering importance and abandoning the desire to reach the goal.* Soon you will discover new secrets of Transurfing that will slightly open the door to this mysterious world of external intention.

The Sail of the Soul

People perceive themselves and the external manifestations of the world only as material objects. All material objects have one informational energy essence that defies regular perception. It is what exists in the space of variations and determines the behavior of material realization. The language of abstract symbols that we are so used to, only describes the external manifestations of informational energy essence. It is impossible to unambiguously describe the actual primary essence by using the language of definitions of the mind. Hence, the vast number of philosophical and religious movements.

Our perception is shaped the way it is, because from our very childhood we have been taught to focus our attention on separate elements at a time. "Look, what a pretty baby! These are your tiny arms, and these are your tiny legs! And this is your yummy porridge! There, look, a little birdie flew by!" Our perception is being tuned throughout our lives. Our mind is constantly trying to bring any external facts into line with the existing *template of the world*.

For example, if we have never seen the energy field of a human being, then our mind won't simply let it reveal itself before our eyes, because it doesn't conform to the usual template. When we were young, no one directed our attention to the aura of a living being. Hence, aura was not part of our template of the world. Now we may know theoretically that the aura exists, but in practice – we won't be able to see anything.

The mechanism of perception of the surrounding world is still a blank spot. We can only discuss its separate aspects. Ants, for example, have never seen the stars. They haven't seen the sun, mountains, or even a forest. Their vision is simply made in such a way that they have only been dealing with near lying objects. Their perception of the world differs fundamentally from our own.

And what does the world really look like? This is an attempt to ask a supposedly objective question and to get an objective answer in return. However, the question itself is not objective. The world *looks just the way we see it*, because the concept of "something looking a certain way" – is also an element of our perception template. In the perception template of, say, a blind mole there is no such concept as "looking a certain way". The world demonstrates itself to us in accordance with our perception template, and at the same time the world *doesn't look* any particular way. There is no point in arguing that the world looks the way it usually does, or like an accumulation of glowing energy, or any other way. There is only sense in talking about its separate manifestations, which we are able to perceive.

The human consciousness is a social product. It is based on the ideas and definitions of everything around us. The soul (the subconscious) resides within any given person from the moment he is born. Yet, his consciousness appears once everything around him is defined and labeled with concepts and definitions in a human language. But the world doesn't exist because people have described it with the help of their own ideas and concepts. In this sense, the human soul will always remain illiterate. She doesn't understand the human language. She only understands what we are used to think of as sensations. First, there is a thought, and only then is it shaped into words. You are able to think without words. And that is precisely the language our subconscious is able to understand. Words are not primary, thoughts are. Trying to speak with the subconscious in the *language of the mind* is pointless.

Far from everything could be expressed by the existing array of concepts. As you may have noticed, I still haven't been able to clearly explain what external intention really is. Fortunately, people still have access to one method of universal expression – works of art. It is something that can be comprehended without using words. Everyone understands *the language of the soul* – it is the language of things that were made with love and desire. When a person is moving towards his cherished goal through the right door – more precisely, when he is doing his thing, he is creating masterpieces. This is exactly how art is born.

You could graduate from a conservatory of music and compose colorless music that no one would even remember. You could make empty paintings that are flawless in their technical execution. However, no one would even think of them as master-pieces. Yet, if someone could say about an object that "there is something about it", then that object could be considered a work of art. Connoisseurs of art and art critics will later explain what that "something" really was. But this "something" is instantly obvious to all and without any words.

Take, for example, the painting *Mona Lisa*. This is the language that everyone understands. Here, words are superfluous. Words are unable to express what is obvious to everyone anyway. And it is not even important what it is that is so obvious to everyone. Every person understands and feels in his own way. One could, of course, say that she has a mysterious smile or that there is something elusive about her, and so on. Regardless, words won't be able to explain "that very thing" that makes this painting a masterpiece.

Mona Lisa sparked such a live interest not only because of her mystique. Didn't it ever occur to you that the Mona Lisa's smile and that of Buddha are very similar? It is believed that Buddha attained enlightenment already in life. In other words, he was able to feel as one with the ocean, much like a drop of water. The smile of Buddha, on all existing images depicting him, is completely dispassionate and at the same time, it expresses calm and bliss. The smile could be described as "contemplating eternity". When you see the smile of Buddha for the first time, there is a strange mix of perplexity and curiosity. This is because it reminds the drop of something distant and forgotten – the feeling of being as one with the ocean.

Any reminder of the past unity pulls sensitive strings of the soul. Once the human language appeared, the language of the soul slowly withered. People got too carried away with the language of the mind. Thus, as time went by, the mind came out on top. Even the account of this process was shaped and distorted by the concepts of mind. I am talking about the legend of The Tower of Babel, where the gods got angry with the humans who decided to build a construction that would reach up to heavens. So, the gods mixed the languages of the people, so they no longer understood each other.

Actually, the majority of myths and legends are true, but it is the mind's version of truth, using his concepts. Perhaps, the tall tower serves as a metaphor that symbolizes the might people once had, having developed the ability to consciously formulate their will in the language of the mind. As it has already been said, *the soul can sense the wind of external intention, but she is unable to set the sail to make use of this wind. The sail is set by the will of the mind. Will is an attribute of awareness.*

The flight of the unconscious soul with the wind of external intention occurs spontaneously, uncontrollably. Mindfulness is what provides the opportunity to purposefully express one's will. At the initial stage, when the languages of the soul and the mind were not as alienated, the unity of soul and mind was relatively easy to achieve. Later on, the mind got carried away with constructing a world view within the context of his own labels and definitions. This, in turn, led the mind further and further away from the comprehension of that initial essence, which underlies external intention.

As a result of gigantic intellectual efforts, the mind achieved impressive results within the technological world of material realization, but he lost everything related to the unrealized space of variations. The mind has gone too far from understanding anything that has to do with external intention. This is why a lot of the claims made by Transurfing seem so incredible. And yet our mind is able to restore what has been lost. You just need to fix the relationship between your soul and your mind.

The difficulty lies in the fact that your soul, unlike your mind, does not think – she knows. While your mind is thinking about the received information, passing it through the analytical filter of his world view template; the soul gets her knowledge directly from the informational field, without any analysis. In exactly the same way, she is able to address external intention directly. In order to make this appeal of hers fit your purposes, you would have to align the will of your mind and the aspiration of your soul, merge them into one. If you were to reach this unity, then the sail of your soul will get filled with the wind of external intention, and it will rush you directly towards your goal.

The Magician within

Your soul possesses everything needed to fulfill your desires. Do you remember the story about the Wizard of Oz and the Emerald City? In that story, the clever Scarecrow dreamt of a brain, the brave Tin Woodman wanted to get a heart, the courageous Lion wanted to get brave, and the girl – Ellie, wanted to go back home. All of these characters already had what they wanted. But if the Wizard of Oz told them, then such a revelation would be too incredible to believe. Thus, the Wizard of Oz pretended to perform a magic ritual.

In fact, all they had to do – the Scarecrow, the Tin Woodsman and the Lion - was only to *let themselves have* the desired qualities, which were already there in their hearts. Ellie's case was not much more complicated – she needed an undeniable determination to have, in order to get back home. The magic ritual helped her to acquire absolute faith, and the wind of intention transferred her back home.

As it has already been mentioned, everything that has to do with external intention does not fit within the framework of the concepts of the mind. He drove himself into this situation, and pendulums helped him a lot in getting there. Having control over external intention provides man with freedom, and that is against pendulums' interests.

They benefit from you being a dullard, a little screw, working for these monsters. Self-realization of any man would be devastating to pendulums, as a free individual doesn't work for pendulums, but for his own development and prosperity. Hence, pendulums make people believe in commonly accepted norms and rules, which turn people into obedient adherents, convenient in use.

On the one hand, there is a positive necessity to teach a person how to normally exist in this world. He, who breaks the commonly accepted norms, becomes a loser or an outcast. But on the other hand, such a suggestion heavily suppresses the individual uniqueness of a person. As a result, people are unable to say exactly what they really want out of life. In addition, they are unaware of what they are capable of.

One only had to separate the mind from the soul, to deprive man of the ability to control external intention. Throughout the entire history of humankind, a great effort was done to separate the soul from the mind. The mind was constantly developing the language of his labels, getting more and more removed from the language of the soul. The pendulums of religion, just as the pendulums of science, were pulling the mind in different directions, but as far away as possible from the actual essence of the soul. The development of industrial and informational technologies in the past few centuries completely disintegrated the connection between the soul and the mind.

The influence of pendulums is now especially great, as everyone is reading books, listening to the radio, watching television and surfing the Internet. Humankind has accumulated a huge amount of knowledge and just as much misleading information. Misleading information bears up just as well as real knowledge. The main loss of humankind is the broken connection between the soul and the mind. Only the chosen few achieve real success in business, science, art, sports and other professional fields. Everybody is used to this being the way of the world, and it doesn't occur to anyone that it is not normal.

There is no point for you and me to "save humankind". I would just like to suggest to you, respected Wanderer, to ask yourself the question: "Why him/her, and not me? What do I need to become one of these few chosen ones?" I am not the Wizard of Oz, so I won't be performing any magic rituals. I will simply give you the answer. *You have everything necessary to become one of the chosen ones. You only have to make use of it. You can do anything. It is just that no one has told you that before.*

You are capable of creating fantastic works of art, making ingenious discoveries, achieving outstanding results in sports, business or any other professional field. To achieve any of that you just need to turn to your soul. She has access to any kind of knowledge, creation and achievement. It is just that you haven't asked any of it of your soul. All great art, science and business geniuses were able to create their masterpieces just because they consulted their soul. *And how is your soul worse? She is not!*

Any masterpiece talks to us in the language of the soul. Regardless of the type of job you are doing, your work will only make an impression if it comes from your soul. Your mind can only assemble a new version of a house, using old bricks. But that won't surprise anyone. Your mind is able to make a flawless copy, but only your soul is capable of creating the original.

All you need – is to take for a fact that your soul is capable of everything, and then let yourself make use of that knowledge. Yes, it is just that easy and inconceivable at the same time. But you should nevertheless allow yourself the luxury to have. The determination to have is only up to you. You are capable of anything.

This claim could raise certain doubts. But you have no doubts when someone is trying to convince you that you do not possess certain abilities, potential or other qualities, that you are unworthy, that others are much better than you are. You easily believe those claims that raise a massive wall on the way to your goal. Then do yourself (not me!) a favor, allow yourself to know that you are worthy of all the very best, and that you are able to accomplish anything that you want with your whole heart.

The actual fact that you are worthy of all the very best and that you are capable of everything, is being thoroughly concealed from your view. You are led to think that it is naive to believe in your unlimited potential. But it is actually the other way around. Wake up and shake off these imposed delusions. The game will run according to your rules, if you will consciously make use of your rights.

No one could stop you from doing this, but common world view and pendulums will in any way possible try to convince you that it is impossible. There will be all kinds of reasonable arguments in favor of your limited potential. Reject these arguments, and add the following "unreasonable and unfounded" argument to your arsenal: *together - your soul and mind are capable of anything.* After all, you are not losing anything by doing so. Have you achieved a lot within the framework of reasonable arguments?

This life is something you have only once. Isn't it time to look over your settled beliefs? They could turn out to be false, and you would never even find out about it. You just wouldn't have the time to find out. Life will pass by, all potentials will be exhausted, and not you, but other people will get all the good stuff this wonderful life has to offer.

Whether you should take advantage of your rights or not, is up to you. If you will allow yourself to have – you will have it. You need to start by believing in the unlimited potential of your soul, and by directing your mind to your soul. False beliefs are in the way of this, and many of these are forced open in the Transurfing model.

One of these false beliefs goes something like this: "The hardest thing is to overcome yourself" or "The hardest thing is to fight yourself". Or take the following sadistic saying: "You must know how to stifle your creativity". This is one of the greatest errors of humankind. How could one and why should one fight such a wonderful, amazing and magnificent being living inside us?! The bad stuff is not living inside us, but on the surface. It's like a layer of dust on a painting. If one were to wipe off the dust, a pure soul would be revealed.

The being that is hiding underneath a multitude of masks and costumes that you wear possesses truly wonderful virtues. *Your task is to let yourself be you.* Have the masks you wear helped you become successful, prosperous and happy? You do not need to change yourself – it will only turn out to be another mask. If you were to drop all your masks, forced on you by destructive pendulums, a treasure hidden in the depths of your soul will reveal itself to you. You are really worthy of all the very best, because you are truly a wonderful, amazing and unique creature. Just let yourself be that creature.

Do you like the creations made by art, science and film geniuses? You could become one of them. You like the works of a genius, because they were brought forth by his soul. Your creation will be liked by others just as much, but only if it will spring directly from your unique soul. Everything that is common and normal was made by somebody's mind. The creations of the mind, just like the mind himself, are not unique. *Only your soul is unique.* You have a real treasure in your possession. Any ingenious creation on your part could only be brought forth by your soul. Have your mind let your soul bring forth ingenious creations.

The Mirage

Throughout his entire life, man is led to believe that success, wealth and fame is something for the chosen ones. When attending educational institutions, competitions, contests and various certifications, it is always made clear to a person that he is far from perfect and that others are better and more worthy than he is. Those, who *refused to believe it,* obtain success, wealth and fame in abundance. That's how simple it is. The only thing that is not simple is *to believe* that anyone of us deserves it and is capable of achieving it. But you really could believe it, if you had the *intention* to do so.

A lot of people want to become a star, to achieve great success. In general, the standard of success is being very actively and widely advocated. Pendulums love demonstrating the achievements of their favorites to the average adherent. Pendulums attempt to present their favorites as a model of success, which one should strive for in order to get all the good things in life. A star gets everything one could have in this life. They bathe in the shine and glory of wealth and fame. Who would say no to that? Even if you do not wish for world wide fame and luxury is of no use to you, it is unlikely that you would say no to being well-off and satisfied, as a result of your own achievements.

Stars are born on their own. But pendulums are the ones to light them up. What I want to say is that the cult of worshipping stars was established and is currently flourishing very much thanks to the pendulums. They are doing it intentionally. In the movies, on stage, in a sports arena, from the television screens – we are constantly being presented with the best of the best, the chosen ones. The way fans are completely ecstatic upon meeting a star, how magnificent the stars are, and their brilliant achievements are especially highlighted by pendulums. We are constantly led to believe one indisputable fact: everyone likes stars, and that is what you should strive for.

What goal are pendulums pursuing, when they are putting their favorites on a pedestal? Perhaps they care about the personal achievements and well-being of their adherents? Absolutely not. They demonstrate the achievements of their favorites, so that the average adherent would be stimulated to work for a particular pendulum even harder than before. After all, how does a regular person turn into a star? Through hard work. Only the best of the best become stars. Anyone could become a star, but you need to work hard for it. Follow their example, do what they are doing, and you too will achieve success. Stars possess unique talents and qualities. Not everyone has them from birth. Hence, you need to work even harder to achieve success.

These are the slogans advanced by pendulums. They do not deny that anyone could be successful, but they are thoroughly hiding the fact that actually everyone, without exception, possesses unique talents and qualities. It would be pure disaster to a pendulum, if everyone were to discover that they possess unique talents. In a situation like that, all adherents would become free individuals, they would get out of hand, and the pendulum would simply fall apart. On the contrary, the pendulum feels best when adherents think and act in one direction. As you may recall from Chapter II[5], uniformity in the thoughts of adherents is the main condition that, if fulfilled, gives birth to a pendulum and allows it to exist. The outstanding personality of a star is an exception, which rather proves the rule, precisely because it is an exception. And that rule reads: "Do as I do!"

That is why a lot of young people get caught in the trap set up by the pendulums. These young people try to be more like their idols, copying them, putting up posters with their idols on in their rooms. The pendulums have their minds on a leash, and their minds blindly follow. The dim-witted mind makes it clear to the soul that the soul is not perfect. It is as if he is telling the soul: "Even I, with my abilities cannot achieve success. There's no way you can do it! But these people – that's a whole different story. See, how cool they are! We must follow their example. So, sit down and be quiet, you with your imperfection, while I'll be trying with all my might to be more like them".

In their attempts to be more like their idols, young people are trying *to catch a mirage*. The aspiration to follow an example and be like those that achieved success – is a job for the internal intention of a fly that is beating against the glass. These young people are tuning into someone else's sector, where they will be nothing more than a parody. The mind is able to create different copies, but you won't amaze or surprise anyone with a copy. A star became the star precisely because of his or her uniqueness, originality and because he or she was different from everyone else. The soul of every person is unique in her own way. A unique soul has her own unique sector in the space of variations, where her exceptional qualities are manifested in all their glory.

Every soul has its own individual "star" sector. It is obvious that there could be an infinite amount of such sectors. But we will consider by convention that there is a unique sector for any given soul – her individual goal or path. The mind, being absorbed with the baits of the pendulums will be muddle-headedly hanging about in someone else's sector, trying to copy someone else's qualities or copy the script of someone else's success. But trying to imitate someone else's script always creates a parody. A soul cannot realize herself in someone else's sector. But how do you find your own sector then? Your mind needn't worry about that, *your soul will find a way to express itself.* The task of your mind is to forget about someone else's experience, to admit that his soul is unique and to let the soul follow her own path.

Teenagers are especially vulnerable to the pendulums' activity, because they have only just entered the world and do not know what to do or how to act. It is easier, safer and more reliable to merge with the crowd, to not distinguish oneself and live like everyone else. Herd instinct provides a feeling of safety, but it nips individuality in the bud. You may notice that the majority of young people are dressed the same, they use the same expressions "cool, awesome, duh..." and they exhibit uniform behavior. Despite the surface polish of independence, they are obediently following the pendulum rule: "Do as I do!" The teenagers themselves think that they carry the modernism of the new generation. But which one of them is *creating* this novelty?

Leaders and outcasts among teenagers are always those few that allowed the unique qualities of their soul to emerge. Developing their distinctiveness, such individuals later turned into those who dictated fashion, set the tone, created new trends, revealed new perspectives and potentials. They did not copy somebody else's experience and they did not obey the rule. Instead, they let themselves realize the unique qualities of their soul. *Pendulums cannot stand individuality, but there is nothing left for them to do but to accept the rising star and make it their favorite.* Pendulums put obvious favorites on a pedestal. These favorites are then presented to average adherents as exemplary.

There is nothing wrong about a boy wanting to become just as strong as his hero. Or that a girl wants to be just as beautiful as her heroines. Just do not copy the things you like about other people. For example, to aim for the exact same set of muscles, exact same way of moving, talking, singing, playing as someone else. You liked this other person precisely because he realized his own unique qualities in his own sector.

There should, of course, be some kind of an original example. Like a demonstration prototype, as long as it is not the model of perfection or somebody you strive to be like. Your perfect model is your soul. Just let her reveal all of her virtues in her own sector. It is better to put your picture on the wall and to admire it instead of some superstar's. Loving yourself is a very good and useful thing to do. Your love towards yourself would turn into complacency and be punished by balancing forces, only if it is followed by despise towards other people.

You really are a unique individual – no one could compete with you in that. Just let yourself be you. You have no rivals in your uniqueness. Keep in mind your right to be unique and you will gain a huge advantage before others who try to copy someone else's experience. Aspiring to be just like somebody else will get you nowhere. Be yourself. Allow yourself this luxury. If you've put on a mask of an already existing star, then it will either be a copy or a parody of that star. You don't become a star trying to be like someone else.

Once you will stop your fruitless attempts of trying to be like somebody else, everything will work out. Once you will stop your fruitless attempts of trying to repeat someone else's script, again – everything will work out for you. Once you will admit to yourself that your individuality is magnificent, others will have nothing left to do but to agree with you. Allow yourself the audacity to have.

All great actors are playing themselves. It would seem odd – their roles are, after all, different. But you can guess that the character, personality and charm, regardless of the portrayed role, belong to one and the same person. The most difficult part to play is that of yourself, letting you be yourself and to take off the mask. To portray another person is easy, because it is much easier to put on a mask. But it would just be an actor's play, a display of professional technique. But to take off a mask is much harder. And if the actor succeeds, then it will no longer be a play but what people refer to as a life on stage.

It only seems difficult. It is actually quite easy to decide to have. You only need to shake off the stereotypes that have been imposed on you by pendulums. And finally, you have to simply start believing in the infinite potential of your soul. Pendulums won't be able to stand in your way, if you were to turn away from someone else's experience and let yourself be a star. Pendulums can only put depressing thoughts in your head like: "A star must be beautiful, and I am not. A star must sing well, play an instrument and dance, and I cannot do any of it. A star must have talent, and I do not have any. I won't pull it off. I have to see how others are going about this."

Indeed, look at music stars, science stars, sports stars, business stars and so on. A lot of them, if not all, do not at all correspond to the common standards and ideas about how a star should be. Every celebrity has lots of flaws, which could overshadow any virtue they have. For example, this superstar has a long nose, and yet she is considered beautiful. And this one cannot carry a tune, and yet everyone is ecstatic about her singing. That actress has no talent for acting, no director would work with her, and still she managed to become a star. This actor is short and fat, what is so great about him that makes him so popular with the ladies? That guy is a nobody – what does everyone see in him anyway? And what about this dull fellow – is he really that guy, that very guy?

It seems as if individuality doesn't fit the rule "do as I do". But wouldn't you agree that it is this particular fact that constitutes the indispensable condition for a star to be born? A bright personality breaks the rule, and pendulums are forced to admit that it is an exception, even though the stereotypes remain in force. All stars are exceptions. And you too will be an exception from the common stereotypes.

You could have a great voice and remain unknown. Or you could be singing terribly, but be original in your performance and people would think you are great. You could have a brilliant and sharp intellect and not achieve a thing. But a miserable no-good that keeps running around with his crazy ideas will sooner or later make a great discovery. You could have impressive physique, but you will never become a sports star. However, he who dares to break the common stereotypes will start playing in a, to him, surprising way, and will emerge a winner. You get the picture. *Have the audacity to direct your mind towards your unique and original soul. Do not be afraid of breaking the stereotypes of pendulums.*

Just don't fall into another trap set by the pendulums. They could provoke you into chasing someone else's goal, which won't bring you anything but disappointment. Why would you need someone else's goal? Listen to your soul, and not to your mind. Your soul knows better in what field you would prove yourself a star.

There is a functioning law in the world of pendulums: only a few become favorites, everyone else has to perform the duties of average adherents and to obey the set rules of the system. Transurfing is unable to break this law, but it can break the law for you in particular, if you should want that. The pendulums would have to make you one of the few favorites, if you were to take advantage of the unique qualities of your soul.

The Guardian Angel

Many believe that a guardian angel is helping their soul. If you believe in your Guardian Angel –great. It means that he exists. You are thinking about him, you put hope in him, you are grateful to him, and these thoughts make him real. Have no doubt about that. Absolutely everything exists in the space of variations. You could even believe that your thoughts create an independent energy being, if that is more convenient to you. The more sincere you are in your love and in expressing your gratitude for the littlest thing, the stronger your little Angel will be, and the more he will be able to help you. In the end, it is not that important whether he exists independently of your thoughts or whether he was made by your thoughts.

Well, there is nothing wrong with not believing in a Guardian Angel. If you feel comfortable without a Guardian Angel, then everything is okay. In the end, you get what you believe in. I would start believing in him, if I were you, because, what if he does exist regardless of your belief? What if he loves you, cares for you in any way he can, and you forgot about him and abandoned him just like that? Thus, he is weak, lacking energy, and is unable to help his charge - you. And at the same time, you are handing your energy to all kinds of destructive pendulums. They can also help you, but only within the limits of their own interests. They do not care about someone's personal well-being. Your Guardian Angel cares only about you.

Imagine him in all possible ways: as a cherub with wings, as a little cloud, a bird or whatever you want to imagine him as. It is not important at all. Your Guardian Angel does not have any appearance on its own. You are the one providing him with a form or shape in your imagination. So, imagine him the way you would feel most comfortable with. You could even equate your Guardian Angel with your soul. If you have psychic abilities – communicate with your Guardian Angel. And if not, then do not worry. He will find a way to put you on the right path. The most important thing to remember is that *you should never resent him and you should definitely not get angry with him.* He knows better what you need to be protected against and in what direction you should go, because in comparison to him - you are like a blind kitten. You are not the one to criticize him. You have no idea what dangers he is trying to keep you from.

There is a tale about a man, who met God in heaven. God showed the man his entire life path, and you could tell by the footprints that God was always walking by the man's side. But then the man got to see the hardest times of his life, and there was only one set of footprints. So, he turned to God, asking reproach-fully "Lord, you abandoned me at the most difficult times in my life!" And God answered: "You are mistaken – it is not your footprints. I was carrying you in my arms."

It is hard to overestimate the role of a Guardian Angel. Already the simple notion that there is a being that cares for you and protects you to the best of his abilities provides you with extra balance in your confidence. And confidence that generates calm and peace plays a major part in a man's life. If you are lonely, you could share your loneliness with your Guardian Angel. If something bad or good happened in your life, you could easily share that with him too. But your Guardian Angel possesses one more property, which you could take advantage of: *unlike you, he is not subject to balancing forces.*

If you take joy in your own success, then you are praising yourself and you are being proud of yourself. That's good. It is much better to praise than to blame yourself. The only bad thing about it is that, while praising yourself, you are creating a small, but excessive potential. Therefore, balancing forces will ruin the celebration of your soul. Having praised yourself, you would later make a mistake or some small annoyance will happen. So, what?

Does that mean that you now have to be afraid of being happy about your achievements, even if you are celebrating in secret?

There is one more way of enjoying your happiness and pride, without creating excessive potentials. *Share your happiness and pride with your Guardian Angel.* After all, he did care for you and helped you on your way to success. He too deserves some praise and gratitude. When you take joy in your success and when you are proud of yourself, remember the Angel and feel happy together. Talk to him. Give him your praise and gratitude. Better to praise him than to praise yourself. You do not have to pretend – sincerely give away your right to the reward. You've got nothing to lose, you've already got what you wanted, and now compliment and say thank you to your Angel.

Think that your success is his achievement. What happens here? Your excessive potential of pride dissolves. And at the same time you can safely leave some space for the party of your soul. Be as happy as you want. *Leave being happy to yourself, and give your pride away to your Guardian Angel.* Because you know anyway that no one can take your achievements away.

Instead of creating excessive potentials of pride, or instead of thanking the pendulum that made you happy, it is much better to give your reward and gratitude to your Guardian Angel. *He is not asking for your energy, but he does need it.* If you think that you got help from a pendulum, you could thank it too – it won't hurt anyone. Just don't forget about your Angel. *Constantly remind him that you are grateful and that you love him.* He will get stronger and will repay you a hundredfold.

A Box for the Soul

Your soul came into this world full of trust and hope, with eyes wide-open. But pendulums hogged your soul at once, and made her believe that no one was waiting for her here, that no one is happy to see her and that she has to do dirty and hard work for a tiny piece of bread. Not everyone, of course, is born in poverty, but the rich have their own problems. They are just of a different kind.

Your soul did not come to this material world to suffer. But pendulums benefit when fighting for your place under the sun becomes normal. As you know, a pendulum that was created by the common thoughts and actions of a group starts living a life of its own, according to the laws of informational energy structure. The pendulum makes its adherents obey it through an informational energy exchange, and forces them to think and act in the pendulum's interests. People are giving pendulums their energy when they express dissatisfaction, irritation, anger, worry, and when they are taking part in battles of pendulums.

We are used to living in this world of pendulums, where depression, hostility, rivalry, wars and other competitive relationships are normal. It does not occur to us that it is not normal, any of it, that it could be different. Look at this world from the point of view of a pendulum. Recall all manifestations of their insatiable thirst for energy, and imagine what the world would look like if it got rid of all its pendulums. If there is no informational energy exchange, then there are no structures that try to make the energy of others their own, giving rise to competition. It is hard to imagine a world without pendulums, but it is safe to say that there would be a lot of happiness and very little suffering in a world like that. In such a world, there would be enough natural resources, riches and opportunities for all.

We have been led to believe that fighting for one's survival and natural selection are two vital normal processes that contribute to further development of life. It is true – processes like that really do promote the development of an aggressive world. However, natural selection is not a critical condition for life to develop. Life could develop according to other, more humane laws.

In the world of pendulums, natural selection follows a negative scenario, according to which *he dies, who is not doing well.* Selection applies the method of repression and destruction. Did it ever occur to you that there could be another, positive scenario? According to a positive scenario, *he survives, who is doing well.* These two scenarios differ in their direction just as the negative differs from the positive. One could argue that both scenarios are at work in the process of natural selection. Yet, nonetheless, the negative continues to be the dominant factor in natural selection: he who isn't doing well – dies. In any case, pendulums have established an even harsher order in the world of man than that in nature.

In nature, the struggle for survival doesn't bear the same fierce and aggressive characters, as in the world of man. The pendulums of people are by far more powerful and aggressive than natural pendulums. The fact that there is always someone eating someone else in nature doesn't mean that there is always a war raging. A lion is eating a cow, just like a cow is eating grass. Animals and plants have no idea about importance, and thus the natural balance is not disturbed. Importance is a property that is only inherent to humankind. When a man is observing natural phenomena from the church tower of importance, he interprets the normal co-existence of living organisms to be a violent struggle.

In the animal kingdom, even competing for territory and partners is of a purely nominal character in comparison to the constant wars raging between the different peoples. Animals very rarely inflict bodily harm on each other, unless they are hunting. In the most cases, any argument is solved in the favor of the animal that had the loudest roar or was most frightening, when baring his teeth. Well, and if blood is shed, then what can you do? Their paws are heavy, after all. Such emotions like malice and hate are not in the nature of animals. Bravery or cowardice is absent as well – there is only the instinct of self-preservation. Brave wolfs and cowardly hares exist only in human imagination.

We cannot change this world in any way. We have to accept things that are not up to us as they are. The myriad of limitations and conditions are literally locking our soul in a box. The mind, captured by all these conditions, becomes a jailer for the soul and does not allow her to realize her talents. Man is simply forced to behave in the way demanded by the world of pendulums: to express dissatisfaction, to be irritated, fearful, and competitive, and to struggle for one thing or another. *The behavior and thoughts of a human being are determined by his dependence on pendulums.* As you have seen in previous chapters, such conditionality takes energy away from a person, turning balancing forces against him and leading him away from his true goals, towards false goals. In addition to everything that has been said so far, external intention is working in realizing our worst fears. And you would be happy to free yourself from conditionality and dependence, but you just do not know how.

Now you know that the power of pendulums lies in importance and unawareness. *Man reacts to the provocations of pendulums, while unaware.* He automatically gives in to anxiety, fear and irritation. He expresses his dissatisfaction and gets angry out of habit. He is easily depressed, and the obstacles on his way make him strain every nerve. That man is living as if in a dream, submitting himself to the script imposed on him by pendulums. He does not realize that he could get his script under his own control. It seems to him that few things are really up to him. Importance draws the man into the game of pendulums, and unawareness deprives him of his last opportunity to exert any kind of influence on his script. *The game is played by the rules of pendulums.*

As you see, I have to repeat the same thing over and over again, because what I am telling you is difficult to grasp or sense, even though it is so obvious. That is how deeply rooted our regular world view is in our consciousness - a world view that has been shaped by pendulums. You could break free from the box of conditionality, if you were to follow the principles of Transurfing. The power of pendulums is great, but they will not be able to stand in your way, if you abandon importance and consciously make use of your right to choose and to define your script.

Pendulums profit from keeping people under control. They only and exclusively pursue their own goals, and to them - man is only but an instrument, a means of getting energy, a string puppet. Your soul came into this world, as if to a celebration – so let yourself have this celebration. It is only up to you, whether you should spend your life working for the benefit of someone else's pendulum, or whether you should live for yourself, for your own pleasure. If you choose celebration, then you have to free yourself from the pendulums holding you down, and find your goal and your door that will lead you to your goal.

Your mind has to understand that you do not have to let destructive pendulums push you around. Unite your mind with your soul, and you will get everything your soul desires, both literally and figuratively speaking. You only need to free yourself from pendulums, and eliminate the dissonance between your soul and your mind. Allow yourself the luxury of being worthy of all the very best.

If someone makes you believe that you have to work for the greater good of something or someone – don't believe him. If someone is trying to prove that to get anything in this world requires a lot of effort – don't believe him. If someone is trying to impose a fierce struggle on you for a place under the sun – don't believe him. If someone is trying to show you where you belong – don't believe him. If someone is trying to lure you into a sect or a society, where it is required that "you contribute to the common cause" - don't believe him. If someone tells you that you were born in poverty, and therefore you must stay poor the rest of your life – don't believe him. If someone is trying to make you believe that you have limited potential – don't believe him.

You shall see for yourself that pendulums won't just leave you alone. As soon as there are a few seeds of determination to have in your heart, pendulums will create a situation where they will try to make it clear to you, in a variety of ways that your potential is limited. As soon as you feel that you are able to choose and define the scenario of the game, pendulums will try to spoil your plans. As soon as you feel calm and confident, they will try to sting you. *Don't give in to the provocations, and don't let them put you out of balance. Keep your importance at a minimum level, and act consciously.* You won't need effort or persistence, but only a conscious intention to keep your importance at zero.

In this game, your potential is only limited by your own intention. The potentials of pendulums are only limited by the level of your impor-tance and the level of your awareness. Remember: if I am empty, they have nothing to hook onto. If I am aware of the meaning of the game, then the pendulums are unable to impose a script on me. If they managed to disappoint you, hurt you, get you out of balance, then you should look back and see where you exceeded your importance.

Change your attitude to that very thing that got you out of balance. Try to realize that it is *pendulums that need your importance, not you.* The box for your soul is made out of your importance. Don't attach excessive importance to *anything.* Just *take what's yours, do it calmly without insisting.* If it doesn't yield just yet, don't attach any significance to it either – pendulums are just waiting for the moment when you'll lose your spirits. If something did bother or hurt you, then remove its importance. Be aware of the fact that it is only pendulums playing. That's right – they are playing, not fighting. It's not a fight of pendulums, as pendulums, are actually like clay dummies.

Their game is cruel, and it is intended for man's weakness. As soon as you slack off in keeping importance at a minimum, you'll get defeated. But if your importance is at zero, then pendulums will fall through your emptiness. The clay dummies will fall to pieces. You'll derive your strength from realizing that you understand the rules of the game. Once you notice that a pendulum is trying to get to you and get you off balance, grin to yourself and keep removing importance. Gradually, such behavior will turn into a habit. That's when you will feel your power. That is when you will understand that you can determine your own game scenario. Having won a victory in the game with pendulums, you will obtain *the freedom of choice.*

Fraile

Up until now, we've been talking about sectors in the space of variations, having certain characteristics – parameters. For the sake of ease, we've agreed to think of these characteristics as frequencies. If the frequency of your mental radiation matches the frequency of a specific sector, given that there's agreement between your soul and your mind, then the force of external intention makes the transfer. In other words, the script and decorations of the given sector are materialized in the layer of your world.

The soul of every person has a unique set of parameters as well – it is called *the fraile* of a soul. Again, to make the model as simple as possible, we'll think of fraile as a frequency characteristic of a person. The fraile of one person differs from the fraile of another person, just like the various shapes of snowflakes are always different, and none is like the other. *Fraile characterizes the individual essence of a person's soul.*

There is no point in developing this definition any further. One could only guess what fraile really is, as fraile is not obvious – it is hidden underneath *the masks of the mind,* which every person wears in one way or another. There is no doubt that any of us possesses some individuality and uniqueness. You could describe the personality, habits, manners and appearance of someone you know, but behind all these characteristics is one integral image that you comprehend without any words. We shall call this particular individual essence – fraile, something that you are able to comprehend without words.

You have probably come across people that possess an inexplicable charm. What's even stranger is that these people could be physically unattractive. However, as soon as one of them starts talking, you instantly forget about his or her physical imperfections, and completely fall for his or her charm. If someone was to ask you what's makes that person so charming, you could only mumble that "there's something about him or her", as you cannot find another explanation. You rarely meet people that are that charming. If nobody you know fits this description, then you may find some of these people among the stars in show business. Their most distinguishing feature is the extraordinary beauty and charm, originating from the depths of their souls. This is not the cold beauty of a doll. You'll notice it right away. The beauty of a doll corresponds only physically to the demands of the established standards.

So, the secret behind charming beauty is not that a given person has a beautiful soul or some kind of spiritual qualities. You will have to accept (or not, as you wish) one more paradoxical conclusion in Transurfing: *there is no so called spiritual beauty. There is only the harmony between the soul and mind.*

If a person doesn't like himself, if he is dissatisfied with himself, if he is doing something he doesn't want to do, or his mind is in disarray, in disharmony with the soul, then he cannot be spiritually beautiful. Any conflict between the soul and mind affects the physical appearance and personality of a person. But if a person is happy with himself, if he loves himself, enjoys his life and if he is doing what he loves, then it is as if he is glowing from the inside. This means that *his mind is set on the fraile of his soul.*

The unity of soul and mind equates the mental energy of a person with the nature of external intention. Being satisfied with yourself, or having your soul and mind in harmony with each other, also creates something similar. The emotional comfort of your soul lights an inner light, which reminds the soul of her true nature. Thus, the beauty of harmony is perceived by people as charm or as spiritual beauty. Such beauty may even make some people envy this glowing person in secret: "How come you are all glowing?"

The soul feels good when the mind is not smothering her in his box, but rather when he is pampering her, like a rose in a greenhouse, looking at her lovingly, carefully nurturing her and letting each little petal of hers to unravel. This is that rare occasion, which we usually call happiness.

Fraile appears as hobbies, interests, everything that is done with love and pleasure. The strings of fraile are often silent for a long period of time. Sometimes, a sign will make the string ring. This could be a random comment that for some reason made something move in your soul. Or it could be something you saw, something that directly attracted your soul in some magnetic way. The attraction you are vaguely aware of will soon appear again and again. That is the external intention of your soul at work. But since it is a vague attraction of the soul - external intention is working with no particular purpose. You need to listen closely to what your soul is telling you to do, so that your mind will pick it up. That's when you will be able to catch external intention, and quickly get what you want.

So, what is standing in the way of your mind to put things right with your soul? The same old importance, and the same old friends – pendulums. They impose false goals and values onto people. As it has been demonstrated before, pendulums are the ones to establish the standards of beauty, success and well-being. Internal and external importance makes a person compare himself to these standards. Of course, his mind finds a bunch of flaws and imperfections, and so the mind starts hating himself and consequently he starts hating the soul as well. The mind tries on all possible masks, trying to fit his fraile into the frame of set standards. Usually, nothing good comes out of that. Thus, the disharmony between the soul and mind is only increased. How could there be talk of the soul feeling comfortable at this point! The mind is watering his rose with blame and dissatisfaction, and the rose is withering more and more.

The mind is going treasure hunting anywhere else but to his soul. The pendulums are sending out loud and alluring invitations, while the soul is only quietly and timidly trying to inform the mind about her abilities and tastes. The mind is not listening to the soul, trying to change her fraile. Obviously, it doesn't lead to anything good. As a result, the soul and mind agree that they do not accept any of their supposed imperfection. External intention transfers the person directly onto the life tracks, where the supposed imperfection is only made worse, because it is being realized in its literal sense.

The mind thinks that if one were to put a corrective mask on, then one could bend to the set standards. As you understand, that is a pointless attempt to catch up to the mirage. Instead of using the precious uniqueness of his fraile, the man is blindly beating against the glass, following someone else's success. But the success of a star was created by the very fact that *its* mind was set on the fraile of *its* soul. The hunter of the mirage fails at his task, and he ends up being even more dissatisfied with himself. *If a man is expressing dissatisfaction with himself, he will never end up on the life tracks, where he is satisfied with himself.* The parameters of his radiations fulfill the conditions of those life tracks, where there are even more reasons for this man to be dissatisfied with himself.

Pendulums impose this meaningless game on people. But this game has a rather specific meaning to the pendulums, as dissatisfaction and discontent – are their favorite energy dishes.

How do you set your mind on to the fraile of your soul? The only way to do it is to convince your mind that your soul has to be loved before everyone else. First, you have to love yourself, and only then notice the virtues of other people. Don't confuse love for yourself with self-love, narcissism and smugness. The latter is created by putting yourself above others, and such an attitude gives rise to the most dangerous excessive potential. To love yourself means to understand your uniqueness and to accept yourself as you are, with all your flaws. Your love towards yourself should be of the unconditional sort, otherwise it will turn into an excessive potential. Aren't you worthy of simply loving yourself? After all, you are the only one you have got.

If a person has gone far in the struggle with his fraile, then he will have a hard time to simply start loving himself. "How could I ever love myself, if I don't even like myself?" Look at the stand the mind is taking: "I love myself, if I like myself." That is excessive potential in its purest form, created by elevated internal and external importance. External importance is elevated in the sense that the standards set by somebody else are the indisputable truth to me. Don't I value too highly the virtues of others? Internal importance is elevated in the sense that I make myself follow someone else's standards. And who said that I'm worse than them? I did, and only I did. Isn't my self-value way too low?

In order to start loving yourself, push external importance off the pedestal, and stop worshipping the standards of others. Who is stopping you from making your own standards? It would be better, if you would let others chase your standards. Drop your inner importance and let go of yourself. You do not have to correspond to or follow someone else's standards. You always have to be aware of the fact that pendulums are the ones that need your importance, not you. Once you start loving your soul with your entire mind, external intention will transfer you to those life tracks, where you will be fully satisfied with yourself. If you will start liking yourself against all odds, you will manage to trick external intention and reveal virtues in yourself that you never thought you had. Once your the energy of your thoughts will start radiating you being satisfied with yourself, external intention will catch you and transfer you to the tracks, where there will really be something to be proud of.

The Golden Rule says: "Do unto others as you would have them do unto you". For some reason, everyone is highlighting the necessity to love others. But the rule implies that you have got love for yourself to begin with. Leave aside the game imposed on you by pendulums, and start loving yourself from this day forward. Buy your favorite treat and celebrate. Look after yourself and take care of yourself. Someone could gloatingly continue: "Indulge in your weaknesses and bad tendencies…" These are the false tales of pendulums, and I think I do not have to enter into a debate with them. You know yourself what it means – to love yourself. Meanwhile, weaknesses and bad tendencies in humans are actually induced by pendulums.

You don't have to look for the Holy Grail somewhere in the jungle. *The Holy Grail is within you – it is the fraile of your soul.*

The Unity of Soul and Mind

The soul comes into this world, and, just like a child, she is trust-ingly extending her little arms. But then it turns out that the world is overrun by pendulums, which turned the world into a jungle. Pendulums immediately try to make the soul believe that there was no one waiting for her here, that in this world – everyone has to fight for their place under the sun and render tribute to pendulums. They immediately want to bring the naive and sponta-neous soul down. She is being told that no one cares for her wishes or desires, that there is more suffering than joy in the world, that there are designated days for holidays, and that you must work hard for a tiny piece of bread. That's it…her little ears drop down, and gloom brings tears to her eyes. Or her indignation grows. This is not right! This is unfair! Her hair is bristling up. It appears to the soul that there could only be one choice: either to, depressed, wander the path forced on her by pendulums, or to desperately keep clawing everyone and everything to get her own way.

Pendulums trap the human mind on three different levels – mental, emotional and on the energy level. The ordinary world view and the behavior of a person are shaped by pendulums. Man thinks and acts just the way that's the most advantageous to pendulums. Following the mind, the soul is put into the box of conditionality. Conditionality is found in almost everything. So, man is forced to accept the numerous limitations and to carry out his assigned role in a forced game. The soul, being in such conditions, is gradually being moved to the background, and the mind takes the reins of government in his own hands.

The mind is teaching the soul, as if it were a little foolish baby: "I know better than you what needs to be done, and your babbling is absolutely useless". In the majority of people, the soul has become this frightened being, deprived of all her rights, sitting in a tight corner and, with sadness in her eyes, watching the mind go wild. It happens sometimes that the soul and mind agree. In moments like that the soul is singing, and the mind is satisfyingly rubbing his hands. But it happens rarely. Most of the time, the unity of soul and mind is attained in not accepting reality, in fear and hate.

The soul does not have the right to her opinion when it comes to making choices. The mind is treating the soul like a child that is asking for a toy she liked in a toy store. The replies of the mind are usually of a standard kind, for example: "We cannot afford that". That is how you destroy the seeds of a dream.

Look at what's happening. The child wants the toy right now. If you really cannot afford the toy, then there is nothing strange about saying no to the child. But the soul is prepared to wait! Nonetheless, the mind, with the conviction of an idiot, puts a fatal end to the discussion: "We don't have any money". Turns out, the dream is basically unattainable.

The mind has his own reasoning that is imposed by pendulums (and they benefit from keeping their adherents on a leash, not even providing them with the freedom of choosing a dream). The soul doesn't have any logic at all – she takes everything literally. The mind keeps telling her that there's no money. But the soul is not asking for money! She is asking for a toy! Yet, the mind puts a ban on the toy (it won't happen, it is hard to get), arguing that there is no money. So, the soul, doomed to a life without the toy, can only withdraw into herself and never again mention the toy. Thus, a dream has been buried.

The mind can't imagine how this dream could be realized. Thus, he doesn't let it into his layer of the world – after all, everything in this life ought to be logical and clear. But he only had to agree to have the toy, and external intention would have taken care of the financial bit and found the money to buy the toy. However, the ordinary world view, shaped by pendulums, won't allow such miracles. The adherents' freedom of choice does not in any way correspond to the interests of pendulums.

Man is wrongly treating the rational world view as an indisputable law. However, this law is a "sham", and it could be "broken". Unexplainable "miracles" often happen in our lives. Then why not let one of these miracles into your life? You only have to let yourself have what your soul desires. If you take off the spider web of preconceptions and limitations that pendulums have ensnared you with, if you will truly believe that you are worthy of your dream, and if you let yourself have the desired – you will get it. *To let yourself have is the main condition of fulfilling a wish.*

There are other answers the mind could tell the soul in a toy store. "Nonsense! I know better what you need. We're simple people. This is impossible. It's not for everyone. You don't have what it takes. You are not talented enough. It's way too good for you. You've got to be like normal people." And so on. If we didn't know that pendulums are responsible for this kind of reasoning, then we could accuse the mind of being completely stupid. But let's hope that, while reading these lines, the mind will nonetheless wake up from the sticky make-belief and will see the entire absurdity of his "reasonable" arguments.

There is very little the mind can do in this world without the soul. Together – they are capable of anything, because if they merge together, they create a magic power – external intention. The mind controls internal intention, and the soul – external intention. Yet, the soul is unable to control external intention with any degree of purposefulness. Once the soul and mind have merged, external intention becomes controllable and it can be used to reach a set goal.

Everything that seems hard to achieve or that seems unreal is really hard to do within the narrow boundaries of a rational world view. And no one is arguing with that. No matter what goal you have set before you, I would agree that attaining that goal will be difficult within the framework of a rational worldview. But you shouldn't reject your dream only because some false authorities have grabbed the right to define what's real and what's not. You too should take advantage of your right to have a personal miracle.

The secret of happiness is just as simple as the secret of unhappiness. It's all about the harmony or disharmony of the soul and mind. The older the person, the greater is this disharmony. The mind submits to the influence of pendulums, and the soul gets miserable. When you are still a child, the soul is still hoping that she will get her toy, but as time goes by, this hope gradually fails. The mind finds all the more evidence that the dream is barely achievable, and postpones its realization. This postponing usually goes on for the rest of one's life. Life comes to an end, and the dream remains in a dusty drawer.

To achieve the unity of soul and mind, first you have to determine what the soul and mind need to agree upon. In other words, you need to identify your goals. Even though this might appear to you as an obvious thing to do, the matter of identifying your goals is far from a triviality. People, generally, know exactly what they do not want, but they have difficulties formulating their true desires. This could be explained by the fact that pendulums are forcing false goals on people and are trying to subjugate them to pendulums' own interests. There can be no talk of any unity of the soul and mind, if the mind is rushing into a chase for an alluring pendulum, while the soul wants something entirely different.

On top of everything else, people are so extremely preoccupied and concerned with doing different jobs for pendulums that they simply do not have the time to sit down and have a good think about what their soul really wants. You have to designate a specific time when you will try to recall what your soul wanted, back when you were just a child. What did you like? What did you want to have? What was really attracting you? And what did you have to give up on, as time went by? Ask yourself the question: is your former goal still as attractive? Think about what you actually want. Could it be that that goal is a false one? Do you really want it with all your soul or do you just *want to want it*?

When you are thinking about your goal, you need to remove internal and external importance. If external intention is elevated, the goal will captivate you with being so prestigious and hard to achieve. Perhaps you've swallowed a pendulum's bait? If your internal intention is elevated, then you might think that reaching this goal is beyond you. The goal is once again attracting you with its inaccessibility. But do you really need that goal?

When you are thinking about your goal, do not think about how prestigious and important it is. Throw the goal off the pedestal of inaccessibility. By doing so, you'll remove external importance. *When thinking about the goal, do not be thinking about ways of achieving it.* By doing so, you will remove internal importance. *Just think about your own comfort.* If the goal has been achieved, do you feel good in your soul? Or is there a weight, sitting heavy on your soul? Having doubts about whether your desires could be fulfilled, does not yet mean that you don't need the desired. The important thing is that when you are thinking about the goal you have long been wishing for, your soul is singing. Even if the goal is all shiny, sparkling and very attractive, if you feel that there's something wrong, then your goal could be a false one. We'll go over all of these questions in detail in the chapter to come.

If you do not have a specific goal and there's nothing that you really want, then – either you have little energy, or your mind has driven your soul into the box completely. In the first case, you could increase you vitality by doing something about your health. Perhaps, you don't even know what it is to be of good health. It's when your life brings you joy and you want everything and you want it at once. There is no such thing as a soul that doesn't want anything at all. After all, to her - this life is a unique chance.

In the second case scenario, you've only got one option - to start loving yourself. Haven't you got too carried away with caring for others? Put yourself in the first place. Others won't get anything good from you, if your own soul is put in the background. By giving away your entire self to serve others, even the people you love, not to mention pendulums, you will waste your life in vain. Your life was given to you not to serve someone else, but to realize yourself as an individual. By locking up your soul in a box, you are creating a massive excessive potential of an inner, hidden dissatisfaction. And it will develop into all possible trouble for you and the people you love. It will seem to you that you want only the good for other people, but in reality - all your caring attempts will bring them harm.

Tend to yourself with care. Treat yourself with interest and attention. Then your soul will warm up and spread her little wings.

Don't believe anyone telling you that you need *to change* to achieve success. You've already heard something like this before, am I right? This is the favorite formula of the pendulums. It's as if they are saying that if you cannot make something work, then you need to do something about yourself. And how do pendulums think you should go about changing yourself? You ought to turn away from yourself, face the pendulums and follow the rule "do as I do", to satisfy their demands and to act in their interests. And in order to change yourself, you would have to fight yourself. How can there be any unity of your soul and mind, if you don't accept yourself, if you don't love yourself, if you are fighting yourself? The soul won't accept false goals. She has her own interests and needs. By chasing false goals, you'll either not achieve anything at all, or, having achieved what you strived for, you will understand that you really didn't need it.

Transurfing is not connected to pendulums in any way, and

that is why it offers a completely different path. Not to change yourself, but to accept yourself as you are. To turn away from the garbage, imposed on you by pendulums and to turn your mind to face your soul. *Listen to what your soul is telling you to do, consciously remove importance, let yourself have, and you will get everything your soul desires.*

To bring your soul and mind together, you need to pay attention to the emotional state of your soul more often. You are feeling comfortable, when there is nothing bothering or putting you down, when you are feeling cozy and calm. Emotional discomfort is the opposite – you're feeling a bit uneasy, something is weighing you down, you are afraid of something, you are down and there's a heavy weight on your heart. If such feelings are very evident and you know their origin, then it is your mind experiencing discomfort. Your mind usually knows what scares him, what worries him or what makes him depressed. You can rely on your mind in a situation like that, as it will provide you with the right solution.

It's a bit more complicated if your soul is the one feeling discomfort, as it is not obvious in its nature. Its feelings are more like a vague premonition. The mind keeps saying: everything is great, everything is running along smoothly and there is no need to worry. And yet, there is something bothering you, despite the rational arguments. This is the rustling of the morning stars. It's not that difficult to hear the voice of your soul. Your only task is to *notice it.* The voice of the mind with its logic reasoning is too loud, and man does not attach any significance to the vague and ambiguous premonitions. The mind, carried away with his logic analysis and prognosis of events, is simply not disposed towards hearing the feelings of the soul.

In order to learn how to listen to the rustle of the morning stars, there is no other way than to develop a habit to pay attention to the emotional state of your soul. Every time you have to make some kind of decision, first – listen to the voice of your mind, and then – to the voice of your soul. As soon as your mind will make a decision, your soul will react to it – in a positive or negative way.

If it is the latter option, you'll have a vague feeling of emotional discomfort.

If you forgot to pay attention to the emotional state of your soul in time, try to later recall what feelings you were experiencing. When you made the decision, you had a passing feeling of something. In that moment, your mind was so absorbed with its own analysis that he didn't have time to consider the feelings of your soul. Now try to remember, what you sensed that very first passing feeling to be. If it was a depressing feeling against a background of the optimistic reasoning of your mind, then your soul clearly said "no".

How much could you trust the premonitions of your soul? If you believe that you are having a premonition about a future event, then you can probably disregard from such a premonition. There is no guarantee that your mind will correctly interpret the information provided by your soul. *The only safe interpretation there could be is your emotional discomfort in reply to a decision made by your mind.*

Emotional comfort doesn't necessarily mean that your soul is saying "yes". It could be that she simply doesn't have an answer. But when the soul is saying "no", you'll definitely sense that. As you know from previous chapters, the soul is able to see sectors in the space of variations. These will be realized, if the decision of your mind will be put into effect. The soul is seeing the results and expresses her attitude towards it – positive or negative. Nevertheless, you could see for yourself, if you gave it a try, that if your soul is saying "no", she is always right in the end.

Thereby, when you have to make a decision, you have a safe criterion of truth – the emotional state of your soul. If your soul is saying "no", but your mind is saying "yes" – go ahead and reject the offer, if it is possible. The soul cannot wish bad things for herself. If your mind is saying "you have to and you will", then you should act as circumstances require. Sometimes in life, you have to accept the unavoidable. In any case, the criterion of emotional discomfort brings clarity and focus to issues where you are experiencing indecisiveness.

Having reached the unity of your soul and mind in regards to your chosen goals, you only have to *attain the unity of determination to have and to act*. Inner intention of your mind must fuse with external intention of your soul. If you are acting within limits of internal intention, and external intention is simultaneously working in the same direction, then you can consider your goal to already be in your pocket. If your internal intention is still a bit unclear, that is when you do not really have a clear idea about how to reach your goal, work on the determination to have instead. External intention is much stronger that internal intention. Thus, it will find a suitable option for you on its own.

It's important that you reach the same unity between your soul and mind in your determination to have that is manifested when you are experiencing strong emotions. The soul and mind usually agree in adoration, contempt and worse fears. We love, hate and fear with all our heart. When the soul and mind are as one – passion is born. "He who cannot hate, won't learn to love", - said the famous Russian writer Nikolai Chernyshevsky.

If the goal has been chosen correctly, then both the soul and mind will be pleased. Your pleasure can only be clouded by the thoughts about that your goal is very hard to achieve or by the narrow zone of emotional comfort. By using slides, you could change the following situation: your mind having doubts about whether it is possible at all, and your soul feeling constrained in "a new chair". You already know how to use slides. Having expanded the comfort zone, you will reach an intense joy of unity, when your soul is singing, and your mind is rubbing his hands, all satisfied.

I'll say this one more time: *when you are thinking about the goal, do not think about how prestigious it is, how unattainable it is and about ways of achieving your goal. Instead, pay attention to the emotional state of your soul.* Are you feeling good or not? Only that matters. In the worst case scenario, you could confuse your soul feeling constrained and your soul feeling emotional discomfort. Constraint or shyness stems from the whole situation being so unusual, as if your soul is saying: "Is all of this for me? Really?"

Discomfort, on the other hand, gives a feeling of depression, that there is a burden to carry, some kind of depressing necessity, gloom, fear and distressing anxiety. If your constraint is not helped by slides, then it is obviously discomfort you are dealing with. Then you should think once again, without trying to fool yourself: do you really need this particular goal?

Sound Slides

A person can belong to one of the three main perception types: visual, kinetic and audio. Some people are more comfortable using visual images, while others are more sensitive to physical sensations, and yet others are particularly receptive to sounds. Until now, we have been talking about slides including visual and emotional images as the most preferable ones.

In some practices of spiritual development, people make use of affirmation techniques. It's where you are repeating the configuration of a specific goal over and over again. For example, take the affirmation: "I have excellent health, potent energy and emotional comfort. I am calm and self-confident". Repeating affirmations aloud or in one's mind is most suitable to people of the audio type of perception. But since there are no pure types, anyone could successfully make use of the affirmation technique.

Affirmations work in the same way as slides. Yet, when practicing affirmations, you have to take into account the differences in the languages of the soul and mind. First of all, the soul does not understand words. If you will thoughtlessly keep repeating something over and over again, it will get you nowhere. The soul only understands wordless thoughts and feelings. Words could to a certain extent model thoughts and feelings, but that's already not it, because speech is secondary to thoughts and feelings. It is much more efficient to feel something one time, than to repeat it a thousand times. Therefore, you have *to strive to experience what you are repeating at the same time.*

Second of all, *any separate affirmation must have a narrow focus.* You shouldn't put several goals together at the same time. For example, the above mentioned affirmation appears to be quite good in content. It contains everything you need. However, while repeating such an affirmation, you won't be able to summon the entire spectrum of the required sensations.

Third of all, you must *avoid monotony and sameness*. Each new series of repetitions should be followed by new aspects of experiences and sensations. For example, if you are constantly repeating the following phrase to yourself: "I am calm and self-confident", these words will soon cease to have their meaning. Confidence appears in the moment when there is the intention to be confident. A desire has to mature, as you keep convincing yourself for a long period of time. Intention, on the other hand, works right away: want to be confident – be confident.

And finally, *you shouldn't direct your affirmations at fighting the consequences,* not having eliminated the cause first. For example, there is no point in repeating: "I have nothing to fear and nothing to worry about", if the cause of your fear and worry is still there. Besides, your affirmation must have a positive tone to it. Instead of the endless repeating of what you would like to avoid, program yourself for the result you would like to achieve. For example, it is better to replace the negative affirmation: "I do not fear and I do not worry", with the positive one: "Everything is working out for me". Be specific in what it is that you would like to work out for you, so that you won't have anything to worry about.

Notice that you need to say "everything is working out", and not "everything will work out". If you phrase your affirmation in the future tense, the future will never become the present, and will instead turn into an oasis somewhere ahead of you. You need to set the parameters of your radiation *as if you already have what you are ordering.*

It's also pointless to order emotional comfort for your soul. The emotional comfort of your soul is a consequence of the harmony between the soul and mind that is achieved in regards to a specific and isolated issue. You cannot achieve this harmony "in general", that is, by the means of abstract self-suggestion. You can only habituate and calm your soul by using a specific slide.

Affirmations have an effect only when you are in a *zero-*

emotional state, when there are no excess potentials. You cannot convince or give orders to your subconscious. When there is any kind of emotional input, you are disrupting the balance. If you are pushing, trying to drum the same thought over and over again into your head, your soul will "shut her ears". The most efficient way to practice affirmations is doing it dispassionately, in a relaxed state. Perhaps then your mind will be heard by your subconscious. However, if your mind is fiercely trying to convince your soul, then he doesn't believe it himself, and no repetitions will dispel his doubts.

You won't achieve anything by having your mind putting pressure on your soul. The determination to have cannot be formed against the background of an emotional arousal. The things you have seem ordinary and natural. Calmly and without insisting, you are simply taking what is yours, as if picking up mail from the mailbox. If you are falsely taking your pushiness to be the determination to have, then you are just spinning around on the same spot, having joined hands with a pendulum. At some point, the pendulum will let go of you, and you will fall head over heels into the pit of former indecisiveness. Yet, once your *determination to have* is free of *the desire to have,* the pendulum will have nothing to hook on to.

As you understand, an affirmation is a kind of *audio slide.* You could use video slides and affirmations just as well. Together – they have the best effect. Here is an example of a complex slide. Let's assume that it contains the image of your new house. You are sitting by the fireside. The rocking chair is creaking. The firewood is slightly crackling. It is so nice to sit and watch the fire! Outside the rain is beating against the windows and a cold wind is howling, but inside it is cozy and warm. There's your favorite treat on the side table. There is an interesting show on TV. You can see, hear and sense it all, and you keep telling yourself: "I am comfortable". You are not looking or listening to the slide, you are living in it instead.

A Window to the Space of Variations

There are all kinds of controlled and uncontrolled thoughts spinning around in a human head. Some call it inner dialogue, but it's actually a *monologue*. The mind has no one else to talk to, except for himself. The soul cannot reason or talk, she can only feel and know. The inner monologue is very loud in comparison to the silent sensations of the soul. Thus, intuition rarely appears and we barely notice it.

There is an opinion that if one were to stop the inner monologue, then the mind will get access to intuitive information. That is true, but it is impossible to shut off the mind completely in a conscious state. Say, you are all concentrated and have thus stopped any passing of thoughts and words. It's almost as if there are no words, there's emptiness inside, but nonetheless it is not the same as stopping the monologue all together. The mind is not sleeping. He is actually doing quite the opposite – he is very vigilant, but he has a different task now – not to think and not to talk. It is as if he is saying: "Alright, I'll be quiet. Let's see what you are going to do next".

This is an illusion. It only seems that the monologue has been stopped. The monologue is stopped, once the mind has shut off his control or at least when he is off guard. But with a false stopping of the monologue, the mind is on his guard and you could say that the feelings of the soul are drowned even more in the "loud" silence of the mind.

If the mind was to shut off his control, your perception would have fallen through into the space of variations. The actual stopping of the mind takes place only in your sleep or in a deep meditative state. The only practical gain one could get from this would be in the case of lucid dreaming or, if you master the technique of deep meditation, where your consciousness is still on.

Lucid dreaming could be used as an interesting experiment and as an opportunity to practice external intention. But could you use the stopping of inner monologue in a conscious state? That's the loophole right there - it constitutes a narrow *window* that is opened spontaneously, when the control of your mind is not as strong, and the intuitive feelings of your soul break through to your consciousness.

Intuition appears as a vague premonition that is also called the inner voice. The mind got distracted, and in that very moment it is easy to sense the feelings or the knowledge of the soul. You've heard the rustling of the morning stars – a voice with no words, contemplation with no thoughts, and a sound with no volume. You have realized something, but it is a vague insight. You are not thinking, but feeling intuitively. Everyone has at some point in their life experienced what's called intuition. For example, you feel that someone is about to drop by, or that something is about to happen, or that you are experiencing an unconscious impulse to do something or other, or you simply *know* something.

When there is a play of thoughts, with the analytical apparatus of your mind as the referee. The mind will quickly sort any data in the label files, so that everything is logical and rational. Stopping the inner monologue would be the same as taking the whistle away from the referee and putting him on the bench. The mind is watching, but now he is unable to control the game.

Juggling with the various data, the mind is making short pauses. It's as if he is taking little breaks to sit on the bench and rest. That's when the window to intuitive information is opened. At times like that you are literally asleep. Perhaps, this may come as a complete surprise to you, but that's how it is. Everyone is falling asleep several times during the day. It's just that they don't notice it, as the window is only opened for a very short period of time.

When you are dreaming, your soul is flying about randomly, so she could be anywhere. In a *window* that has been opened in a conscious state, your soul is focused on a specific sector in the space of variations, in contrast to her random whereabouts in a dream. This sector is related to the thoughts going through your mind at that moment. Thus, the context of your thoughts directs the gaze of your soul at the corresponding sector in space. There the soul will see the knowledge that is related to the present content of your thoughts. As soon as the window is opened, this knowledge breaks through to your mind. If the awakened mind pays attention to the impressions of your soul, i.e. if he remembers this short flash of his dream, then he will obtain the very thing that is called intuitive knowledge.

It is usually assumed that intuitive enlightenment is a spontaneous flash of insight in your mind. On the one hand, a decision suddenly downs on your mind "from above", and on the other hand, it is claimed that your mind found that decision on his own. What is then the origin of this "knowledge out of nowhere"? Ordinary worldview overlooks this strange fact and discounts it, by saying that that's the nature of our mind.

We can see from the model of Transurfing that the mechanism of enlightenment is of a completely different nature. The mind finds his conclusions by the means of logical reasoning. Yet, enlightenment, the missing link that could never be obtained from the present logical chain of information, comes to you from the space of variations with your soul as the mediator.

The vague feelings of your soul appear as anxiety, depression or inspiration and enthusiasm. All these feelings could be described with one word – languish. It is as if the soul is trying to convey something to the mind, but is unable to explain it. Agonizing anxiety, feelings of guilt, the burden of duty, depression are realized as your worst fears. The soul and mind agree on all of these feelings. Our worst fears are realized because of external intention and the work it is doing.

You know that when it rains, it pours. Having parameters of radiation such as these, we are being transferred onto the worst life tracks where, as they say, when it rains, it pours. Sometimes, an induced transfer drives us into a dark period of our life, and it takes us a long time to get out of it. You could notice that when you are in low spirits, your worst fears are instantly realized. External intention transfers you onto unfortunate life tracks, where the situation is getting worse virtually in front of you.

The soul, in parallel to sensing trouble, is actually helping to realize the impending trouble, as she is contributing to the unity of the soul and mind. By applying this unity to your best expectations you could turn external intention to your benefit. That's why Transurfing suggests that you reject importance, reject the negative and that you consciously direct your mental energy at achieving your goals. As you already know, slides help setting the parameters of your mental energy, and you should use slides in a conscious state of mind. The same method could be used in the moment of the open window, if you manage to capture that moment.

Intuitive knowledge and premonitions occur spontaneously. In this case your mind is passively making use of the potential of your soul – he simply gets the information from the sector, where the soul happens to be at that moment. So, our task is *to be able to intentionally summon intuitive premonitions.* This should be done in order to turn the sail of the soul in the right direction.

How should this be done? You must seize the moment when the mind is distracted. Only now, you do not have to try and sense the feelings of your soul, instead – you should deliberately induce these feelings. That is, you should put a momentary slide into the open window. The slide must contain the feelings that you experience inside the slide. When you are putting the slide into the open window, you are not getting any information from the soul; instead you direct the soul into a special sector in the space of variations. If you manage to do this, your mind will touch upon external intention.

It would seem that a similar effect could be obtained if one were to play the slide before falling asleep, while lying in bed. Then the slide would softly turn into a dream, and the unity of your soul and mind would be obtained. Yet, as strange as it may seem, that won't work. I'll tell you why in the upcoming section. Meanwhile, try to answer the question: *why is there no point in playing a slide in your dream?*

Frame

There is a transitional area between events that have been formed by external intention, and the events that have been foretold by intuitive feelings. In other words, when you sense that something is about to happen, you touch the event with your thoughts in passing, without further intention to do so. This event is usually realized, especially if the mind agrees with the intuitive feelings of your soul. So here's the question: did you only sense that something was about to happen, or did your subconscious thoughts act as external intention and induced this event?

There is no simple answer to this question. Both things happen. In a dream, there is more certainty about what's going on: should you only think about something in passing or rather sense that an event will develop in a certain way, as it is instantly realized. External intention in your dream works without a hitch. So what's in it for us?

Only that we get the realization of an expected scenario in a dream. *A dream has no effect what so ever on physical reality.* Virtual reality will remain as such. Then why won't external intention of a dream realize a virtual sector? It would seem that it has something to do with the inertness of our physical reality.

Indeed, to compare a dream to physical reality is like comparing a little paper boat to a large frigate. The little paper boat is rapidly flying away at the tiniest breath of external intention. But in order to move the heavy frigate, you need a large sail and a prolonged period of time.

And yet, it is not just inertness that keeps the external intention of a dream from realizing a virtual sector in physical reality. You could play your slide all you want, you could even play it in a lucid dream, but it won't get you any closer to your goal. The point is that external intention has only one function in a dream: to transfer the soul from one virtual sector to another. This is what happens in a dream: the mind has set the feather sail of the soul in accordance with his expectations, and external intention instantly transferred the little paper boat into the corresponding sector. That's it. The job is done, and the mission of external intention has been completed.

In reality, the work of external intention is not completed with only a breath. The wind of intention is blowing, but the frigate is not moving. If the unity of the soul and mind has been attained, the sail is set in the right direction. The size of the sail depends on the degree of this unity. The wind cannot instantly transfer the frigate to the right sector. The parameters of energy of mental radiation already comply with the sector of your goal, but the material realization is delayed in an earlier sector. Thus, the wind of intention must blow for some time in order to realize the sector of your goal.

However, the external intention of dreaming cannot make the frigate move at all, simply because there is only the feather that has been set on the paper boat. The sail of the frigate was *put away. The wind of intention is only able to move the little paper boat of dreams, but has no effect on the frigate of material realization.*

Thus, playing the slide in your dream does not contribute to the movement of material realization. The sail of your soul in a dream allows your soul to fly about in virtual space, but it has actually nothing to do with the movement of material realization. The only function of a slide in a lucid dream is to expand the comfort zone of your soul. And that's already something. So, if you are practicing lucid dreaming, then the slide in your dream will be an ideal way to expand the comfort zone of your soul.

When you are awake, your consciousness and subconscious are within limits of the physical world. The mind is keeping the general course of your soul within the sector of material realization. As it has already been demonstrated above, the mind is constantly adjusting perception in accordance with the set stereotype. When you are awake and playing the slide in your mind, you are setting the parameters of your mental radiation onto a sector that has not yet been realized. Depending on the degree of unity your soul and mind experience towards your goal, your sail starts filling with the wind of external intention and the frigate slowly and gradually starts moving into the sector of your goal. The work of external intention is done, once the material realization has arrived at its destination.

Do you see the difference? The work of external intention in a dream is coming to an end, while it continues when you are awake. In a dream, the parameters are instantly brought into conformity with your desires, and that's it. Yet, in reality, it is a slow and gradual process. *When you are awake and playing the slide, the sail of material realization has been set, and so – external intention is moving the frigate, and not the little boat of dreams.*

Do not be disturbed by the fact that I am using simple metaphors to describe all of these complicated questions. There are no better suitable analogies on the list of labels of our mind anyway, but the essence of it all is communicated more clearly this way.

The window into the space of variations, opened in the brief moment when the mind is falling asleep, leaves the focus of perception in the *context* of current material realization. In contrast to an ordinary dreaming session, the sail of the frigate in the window remains raised. If you were to put a slide in the window at that precise moment, then the gust of wind of external intention would move the material realization a significant distance. The efficiency of the window lies in the fact that the unity of the soul and mind is at its peak in the moment of the open window. The dozy mind lets go of his control, and lets in the unreal in his model of perception, much like he does in a dream. The sail of the soul assumes considerable magnitude, and external intention is acting with the greatest of power.

This method is rather difficult, but you could try it. You should start with always paying attention to your intuitive feelings, observing yourself. Then you will realize that the window is being opened quite a few times during the day. From time to time, the mind gets tired of his own chatter and being in control. Thus, he loses his vigilance for a moment. In that moment, you could intentionally put the feelings you have about an event you'd like to induce, into the window. It has to be feelings, and not phrased words.

Imagine what you would feel, if what you wished for came true? Play the slide of reaching your goal in your head a few times, and then take one integral cast from the entire slide which we will call *a frame*. For example, you sign the contract and feel satisfied. Or you successfully pass an exam, and the lecturer is shaking your hand. Or you finish first and tear apart the ribbon with your chest. This cast will be that formula, which you will have to put into the half-open window. The frame could have a one word title, for example: "Victory!", "Yes!", "Great!" or whatever you prefer. This heading will be the reference point of the frame.

It's difficult to catch the window, because it is your mind that has to do it, even though it is dozy, which means that the mind wakes up upon catching the window, and the window is instantly shut. You'll gradually get the hang of it. You need to have a firm intention and patience. First, you need to develop a frame of sensing an event being realized with the help of your mind. Let him actively take part in this process of development. Then, without trying to catch the window, play this frame so that you firmly establish the true nature of the feelings you will experience upon reaching your goal. Create a hook, the essential sensation. And then, you could try to instantly put the frame into the open window when the opportunity arises.

This is what should happen – your dozy mind must realize that he is dozing and instantly throw the frame into the window, not having wakened up just yet. This is what the function of external intention will be, when the inner monologue has been paused.

The many, although unsuccessful, attempts will gradually form a habit, and your mind will learn to automatically throw the frame into the open window. The idea behind the frame is exactly that the mind should be able to activate it automatically without being awake yet.

However, if the method of frames is very difficult to you, don't get disappointed, and leave it alone. This method is mentioned here only for the sake of information. If it doesn't work the first time, then you don't need it. Keep working with the usual slides and keep visualizing the process.

In any case, it would be rather useful to make a habit out of paying attention to the windows. If you learn to catch the moment of an open window, intuitive insights will be more frequent in your life.

Summary

The mind has a will, but he is unable to feel external intention.

The soul is able to feel external intention, but does not have a will.

The unity of your soul and your mind submits external intention to your will.

Your soul is not in any way worse than the souls of others. You are worthy of all the very best.

You have everything you need. You only have to make use of it.

Stars are born on their own. But pendulums are the ones to light them.

Pendulums conceal the fact that each and everyone have unique abilities.

The rule "do as I do" creates the generally accepted stereotypes of pendulums.

Every soul has its own individual "star" sector.

If the mind will let her, the soul will find the right sector on her own.

Allow yourself the audacity to believe in the unlimited potential of your soul.

Allow yourself the audacity to have the right to your fantastic individuality.

Leave the joy to yourself, and give your pride to your Angel.

The behavior and thoughts of a person are defined by his dependence on pendulums.

Keep your importance on a minimum level and act consciously.

Do not attach excessive significance to anything.

You do not need your importance, pendulums do.

Conscious intention, but not efforts and persistence, keep importance on zero level.

Fraile characterizes the individual essence of a man's soul.

The mind gets further and further away from the soul, chasing the standards of others.

Having set your mind on the fraile of your soul, you will get a whole lot of hidden virtues.

When your soul and mind are united, your soul is singing and your mind is rubbing his hands with satisfaction.

The mind, thinking about the means of achieving the goal, puts a fatal end to the barely achievable goal.

Letting yourself have - is the main condition of fulfilling your wishes.

If you feel that there is something not right about the goal, no matter how appealing it is, the goal might be a false one.

Do not believe anyone who urges you to change yourself.

You can tell that your soul is experiencing discomfort, when you feel distressed, depressed or when you feel like you have a burden to carry.

The emotional comfort of your soul is not an obvious "yes".

The emotional discomfort of your soul is an obvious "no".

Thinking about the goal, do not think about how prestigious and unattainable it is, or about ways of reaching the goal. Heed only to the state of emotional comfort of your soul.

An affirmation must be followed by appropriate feelings.

A separate affirmation must be positive and targeting.

Direct your affirmation at the cause, and not at the consequence.

Phrase your affirmation in the present tense.

When your determination to have is deprived of any desire, the pendulum has nothing to hook onto.

Calmly and without insisting, you are picking up your mail from the mailbox.

CHAPTER IV

GOALS AND DOORS

Each person has their own path where they will gain true happiness. But how do you find this path? You are about to find out. And since your desires do not always match your possibilities, how do you reach the goal you have set before you? You shall see for yourself that your possibilities are only limited by your intention. By breaking the locks of stereotypes, you are opening the doors that previously seemed inaccessible.

By forcing the locks of stereotypes, you are opening doors.

How to Choose Your Things

In this chapter, we shall talk about how to distinguish the genuine aspirations of our soul from the false goals, imposed on us by pendulums over and over again. The problem is that no matter how attractive a false goal may be it will not bring you personally anything but disappointment. Either you won't achieve anything at all in your pursuit of the false goal, and all your efforts will end up feeding pendulums, or, having reached the goal, you will realize that you actually didn't need the goal at all. Is it worth missing a unique opportunity that was given to you in life, and waste precious time on correcting mistakes? Even though it may seem that a life is a long time, it goes by very quickly and unnoticeably. Thus, you need to know how to find goals that are truly yours, the goals that will bring happiness to you personally.

I would not want to begin this chapter with theory. You are probably already tired of the complex theoretical bases. To the best of my abilities, I've tried to make the heavy account easy to understand, but I'm afraid I haven't always been successful. What can you do? After all, we've touched upon some rather unusual questions, and the conclusions have been all the more astounding. Your mind would have never taken any of the Transurfing ideas seriously, if I hadn't provided you with at least some kind of theoretical basis. But the most complicated stuff is now behind us, and thus, I shall begin this chapter with matters of practical nature.

Looking for clothes, is the most striking and simple example of how to choose ones goal. And it can also be used to practice one's goal choosing skills. You can probably recall a few times when you've bought something that seemed appropriate, but then it so happened that you stopped liking that item or it no longer fitted you, or there was something wrong with it. And then there have been times when you've seen a piece of clothing, and bought it straight away and you are still happy with it. The difference between these two items is that the first one belonged to someone else, and the second is yours.

The first item that seemed appealing to you was intended for another person. Perhaps, you saw one of your friends or a model wearing it. If an item looks good on someone else, it does not yet mean that it will look good on you too. And it is not a physical flaw of your body, but rather an asset. It is very bad to be a model on whom everything looks good. It is not the generally accepted beauty that makes a strong impression but rather a finely accentuated individuality.

I know that you didn't need me to tell you that. But you do spend a long time shopping and agonizing over not knowing what to buy. Knowing the different styles, having an eye for fashion and even good taste doesn't help. After a long search you are still not quite satisfied with your purchase. To always find exactly what you need, you would have to learn how to distinguish your things from the things that are meant for other people. So how do you do that? You won't believe how simple it is!

First of all, never agonize over the problem of choice. It's obvious that the balance is being upset in a situation like that. The more you strain yourself in this regard - the worse will be the outcome. There is no need for you to examine the different items for a long time and to analyze what's good and bad about them. Your mind should not take part in your choice making, as your mind and his thoughts – is not you, but a coating left over from the influence of pendulums. Just walk and look around you, as if you were on an exhibition, not thinking about anything.

To begin with, identify in general terms what you would like to get. You do not have to picture the details. The only description you need is what type of clothing you would like to get. For example, if you need a coat, simply make it your goal to choose a coat, and that is it – no more unnecessary conditions. Let the soul choose the item – your soul is actually much closer to what you are. She won't miss a single detail and will surely indicate the right item at the right time. As soon as you see or rather feel particularly drawn towards an item in the sea of clothes, you will instantly realize that you have spotted the right thing.

I would like to point this out one more time – you do not have to analyze why that particular item appeals to you. You just like it and everything you could say about it would be: "This is what I need". You'll buy it without further reasoning.

Even if you have already been looking for a long time and cannot find anything that you like, do not worry, your item will be in some store or other. It may not be in the third shop, but it maybe in the tenth. It is patiently waiting for you, so be patient too. Don't rush about, don't torture yourself with doubts and don't reproach yourself. To make you absolutely sure, I'll reveal to you the secret behind telling someone else's item from your own. It is just as simple, as it is reliable.

As I've already mentioned, while you are in the process of choosing things, you shouldn't be thinking about what's good and bad about these. But then the moment has come for you to either say "yes" or "no" to the shop assistant. In that moment you are sleeping very soundly, even if it may seem to you that this is not the case. Your sleep is particularly heavy when the shop assistant or your friend is telling you something about the item in question.

While you are making a choice, there is only your mind at work. He is analyzing the pros and cons, arranging his conception so that it would be rational and convincing, and at the same time he is listening closely to the opinions of the people around you. Your mind is so absorbed in this process that he doesn't at all notice the feelings of your soul. In that sense your mind is sleeping soundly.

Well, and let it sleep. Don't disturb him until he has made a choice. But now the decision has been made. Don't listen to anybody in that moment, *wake up and become aware of the following: what feelings did you experience when the decision was made?* The state of emotional comfort of your soul will show the attitude of your soul towards the decision that has been made by your mind.

As you already know, the emotional comfort of your soul cannot provide you with a definite answer. You soul doesn't always know for sure what she wants, and so she could also be hesitating. If you liked the item from the very first sight and you sensed that right away, then your soul said "yes". But then your mind joins in and starts analyzing and substantiating your choice. If, having analyzed the situation, your mind said "yes", then the item is yours. But if you decided to buy that particular item because it is worthwhile buying, and not because you liked it from the start, then you should pay special attention to the smallest discomfort your soul might be experiencing. *Your soul always knows for sure what she does not want.*

If you are hesitating, if there is anything about that item that makes you a little uneasy or worried, if there is the slightest shadow of doubt or gloominess – then it is someone else's item. Your mind will be trying to persuade you, and describing in glowing terms everything that's good about that particular item. If you catch yourself *persuading* and trying to convince yourself that the item fits you both in style and size – then you can throw that thing away at once and without regret: it is not yours.

The definite criterion of choice fits within this simple phrase: *if you have to persuade yourself, then it is someone else's item.* Know this: that *if the item is yours, you won't have to persuade yourself.*

Well, and finally, should you listen to the opinion of others, while you are in the process of choosing your items? I don't think you should. No one, except for you can choose an item that is actually yours. If you absolutely liked the item, then you can be entirely sure that others, having seen you wear that item, will think it's great too.

There is only one thing I can say about prices: your item doesn't at all have to be located in expensive shops. But if anything, Transurfing will help you remove the money problem from your life. If you define *your goal* and strive towards *it*, and not towards having more money, then the money will come to you on its own, and you'll have more than plenty of it.

As you see, the process of choosing one's things includes all of the main principles of Transurfing. You are shopping, as if you were on an exhibition, simply observing and not making it your goal to find something no matter what. Consequently, you are rejecting the desire to reach the goal. You are calmly becoming aware of the fact that your item is waiting for you someplace, and you know for sure how to tell it apart from someone else's item. Thus, importance is at a minimum level. You wake up right after the decision has been made, and you become aware of the entire process. Thus, you are acting consciously and you are the one determining the scenario of the game. When making the final decision, you are relying on the state of emotional comfort of your soul. And you won't be wrong, because there is a tower of strength in this unstable world – it is the unity of soul and mind. And, finally, you will make things much easier for yourself, if you rely on the flow of variation, instead of doing strict planning, binding yourself up with the circumstances and having your way no matter what. Life – is a light celebration, if you let yourself have it. Take what's yours, calmly and without insisting.

Well, that is it. Now you know a simple and powerful method. You can calmly go to a shop, and even if you don't buy anything that day, you've saved yourself from buying somebody else's item. You will be calm and confident, because you know that your item is lying somewhere, waiting for you. And you will definitely find it. The important thing is – not to forget that before saying "yes" or "no", you need to wake up and become aware of your sensations.

When you are buying clothes for someone else, for example a child, then this particular method won't work. Actually, it does work, but not with the same high level of precision there would be, if you were buying clothes for yourself. Your soul won't be able to choose an item that is intended for someone else. Thus, you can only be governed by practical considerations. Yet, at the same time, give the child the opportunity to choose his clothes himself. Children, unlike adults, are able to find their items.

Of course, this method is not restricted to choosing clothes only - you can use it whenever you need to pick something out for yourself. And I would really like to hope that the book you are holding in your hands - is yours.

How to Dictate Fashion

Would you like to become a trendsetter? After all, before, the only thing left for you to do was to pay attention to the way others were dressed, and try to keep up with the latest fashion trends. Yet, have you considered who is creating this fashion? Fashion is not born in the salons of the leading fashion designers – they only pick it up. New fashion trends are made by people that are relatively free of pendulums. These people are governed only by their own independent judgments and preferences, and that is how they become fashion trendsetters. They dress the way their heart is telling them, and they hit the bull's eye. Later, that particular idea is noticed by others. It is thus picked up and continues to spread spontaneously.

If one were to blindly follow the latest trends, then one could completely spoil one's looks. If you were to watch how people are dressed, you would notice a few elegant people that are not fashionably dressed. But, you notice immediately that there is something about the way they are dressed, and it doesn't occur to anyone to accuse them of being unfashionable. And the other way around, you constantly stumble upon creatures that are dressed according to the latest trends, but you just feel sorry for them, because it doesn't suit them at all. The imitators are blindly walking along the path of inner intention towards someone else's goal that was determined by the pendulum of fashion. They do not stop to think about their own preferences and they submit to the rule of pendulums, "do as I do". Here I'd like to recall a French saying: "Don't be afraid of looking unfashionable – be afraid of looking ridiculous".

On the outside, fashion is about style, yet its inner substance – is what suits you in particular, in the context of the given style. You just need to have a clear idea about what you want: to look trendy or to look elegant? It is not the same thing. And what do you think is a better option? One could dress up in some retro clothes that are completely out of date. But if it is your thing, then everyone will get green with envy.

You have probably already guessed that following fashion trends is nothing other than taking part in the game of the fashion pendulum. Fashion trends quickly appear and then just as quickly disappear. It is one of the more short-lived pendulums. It is no big deal if you find yourself under the influence of a fashion pendulum. Make it your goal to look interesting and elegant. You do not have to be specific about any details. Just walk around in the different shops and examine the clothes by practicing the above mentioned method. Forget all about current fashion trends. Pay attention only to your feelings, which you experience when looking at a particular item. Turn off your analytical apparatus; stop thinking, evaluating and reasoning all together. As soon as you catch yourself trying to reason and analyze, immediately stop this pointless process. Listen to the rustling of the morning stars.

It is most likely that it won't work right away. Give yourself an undefined amount of time and reject the desire to realize your goal. After all, if it doesn't work out, then it is not like you will be losing anything. Free yourself from the responsibility to achieve the goal. Drop importance and loosen your grip. Just walk around and look at the different pieces of clothing, try them on for curiosity's sake. Rely on the flow of variations.

It will be useful to at the same time play the slide of your goal in your mind. However, it should not be a specific image of what you look like. The slide must consist of sensations that you are experiencing when you attract attention and look elegant, interesting and original.

Abandon the desire to find something extravagant, something that sticks out. Just because a thing appears to be extraordinary, it does not yet mean that it will bring you the desired effect. Trust me, you are already about to make several surprising discoveries as it is. After a while you will definitely discover an original and innovative solution. As soon as your soul and mind have been united, you will experience a feeling like no other. It will be a mix of surprise and joy. You will realize it right away, but you won't say to yourself: "That's what I need". You will want to exclaim something like: "It can't be! Fantastic!" That's the way it is. Your possibilities are only limited by your own intention.

The secret of success lies in the fact that you have freed yourself from the influence of pendulums and gone your own way. And what do pendulums do when they see that a new star is rising in the sky? As you know from the previous chapter, they light it. There is just nothing left for them to do than to make you a star, their favorite. Pendulums attempt to keep everything under control, thus they will even help you to achieve your goal. And if you are lucky, you will create your own pendulum and become its favorite.

Everything that has been said so far does not only relate to clothes, of course. The same principles could be applied to everything you do. It is a magnificent privilege – to be yourself! And that is exactly the privilege that any man could afford. But only a few dare to. There is only one reason to why that is the case – heavy dependence on pendulums. They need obedient puppets, and not independent individuals. The only thing left for you to do is to understand that, to free yourself from the unnecessary influence and become yourself.

In other words, your mind must put the following simple truth onto the list of his labels: *everyone possesses a precious treasure – the uniqueness of their soul.* Every person carries within him a key to success and yet, he does not use it. Let your mind take your soul by her little arm, lead her to the store and let her choose the toy herself.

The unity of your soul and mind – is such a rarity that it could literally be sold at a profit. All of the masterpieces of culture and art – is a manifestation of this unity. The stars will remain the stars only because people are interested in what they lack themselves –

the unity of soul and mind.

The Goals of Others
Up until now we have been examining the outside world as a space of variations with sectors that are bundled into life tracks. If the parameters of mental radiation energy correspond with the parameters of a particular sector, then the sector is manifested in material reality. Yet, on the energy plane, the man himself is an individual being that has a unique spectrum of radiation. Each individual has "his own" life tracks in the space of variations, life tracks that are more suitable for the fraile of his soul.

Being on one of his life tracks, a man would encounter minimum obstacles on his way, and all circumstances would be favorable. The fraile of the man's soul successfully fits into his own life track and he achieves his goal with ease. In the exact same way, the home key is easy to turn in the lock and thus, it opens the locked door. We do not need to know exactly how and why all of this happens. The only thing that matters is the actual fact that every person has his own path, his own door. If a person is walking towards his goal through his door, everything turns out well for him.

In the worst case, if a person has turned away from his path, all kinds of misfortunes fall on his head and his life turns into a constant struggle for survival. It is a real tragedy for your soul. After all, you do get sad if it's bad weather on your day off, right? You can imagine what your soul is feeling, when a unique chance, given to her by this life, is wasted.

The soul sees how the mind, carried away by pendulums, ruins his own life, but she cannot change anything. The mind, when entering the world, does not know for sure what he needs to do, what to want, what to strive for. The soul, if she doesn't know for sure, then she at least can have some clue about all these things, but the mind doesn't listen to her. Pendulums immediately take the mind in hand, imposing their goals and rules of the games on him. They make people choose the goals of others and make them crowd at someone else's doors. The weak attempts of the soul to influence the mind are all in vain. That is how strong the influence of pendulums is.

Many of us have been instilled from our very childhood with the thought that success can only be achieved through hard work. And what's more, you have to persistently keep on walking towards your goal, overcoming obstacles. One of the greatest mistakes is the idea that you have to fight for your happiness; that you have to show persistence, perseverance and you have to overcome a lot of obstacles. Basically, you have to conquer your place under the sun. This is a very harmful and false stereotype.

Let's figure out how such a stereotype might have been formed. Usually, a man would get under the influence of pendulums and turn away from his own path. Obviously, in a case like that he is bound to encounter a lot of obstacles. But he wants to achieve happiness, and so he is forced to overcome these obstacles. Try to guess, what is his mistake? Is it, perhaps, that he is walking towards someone else's goal through someone else's door? No. The answer will again seem surprising to you, as everything else in this book.

The mistake of this man lies in his false conviction: "If I overcome obstacles, then there, ahead lies happiness". It's nothing more than an illusion. There is no happiness ahead! No matter how much he tries, he will always be the one chasing the setting sun. *There is no happiness for a person on someone else's life track. Not in the near, nor in any distant future.*

A lot of people, having reached their set goal through a great deal of effort, don't feel anything but devastation. Where did that happiness go? It wasn't there to begin with. After all, it is a *mirage,* created by pendulums in order to make you give them your energy on your way to illusory happiness. I say it one more time: *there is no happiness ahead. It is either here and now, on the present life track, or it is not there at all.*

What is happiness according to the model of Transurfing? Perhaps, it will come, if one were to achieve one's own goal? Wrong again. *Happiness comes while you are moving towards your goal through your door.* If a man is on his own life track, on his own path, then he is already happy, even if the goal is still ahead of him. That is when life turns into a celebration. Once the goal has been reached, it will be a double joy. However, actually moving towards your goal is already turning each day into a celebration. *Moving towards someone else's goal always leaves the celebration in the illusory future. Achieving someone else's goal brings disappointment and devastation, but it will never bring you happiness.*

Your goal – is what brings you true pleasure. It is not what brings you temporary satisfaction, but rather something that *gives you a feeling of joy of life.* Your door – is the path that leads you to your goal. You should be experiencing enthusiasm and inspiration on that path of yours. It's not that everything comes easy on that path. The main thing is that moving through your goal *does not devastate you, but brings you a new burst of energy instead.*

If you are walking towards your goal through your door, the obstacles are easily overcome, and any effort on your part isn't really of any burden to you. If, however, you strain every nerve, if you are uninspired in your work and get tired on your way to the goal, then that is either someone else's goal or you are trying to force your way through someone else's door. Let's note the characteristic features of goals of other people.

The goal of another person – it is always forcing yourself and making you do things. It is an obligation. If you find even the *slightest forced necessity* in your goal, then you can go ahead and abandon it. You won't have to persuade yourself, if the goal is yours. Walking towards your own goal is a pleasant journey. The process of its achievement brings you joy. When you are walking towards someone else's goal, you are overcoming a lot of obstacles. The way to someone else's goal is always a struggle. A pendulum needs for everyone to neatly do their job of a small cog in the wheel, for the good of the entire mechanism. You are struggling, but you will keep doing it, because pendulums have made you believe that the only way to achieve anything is through hard work. If you are cool, you must overcome yourself, overcome any obstacle that you may encounter, go through fire and water, and conquer your place under the sun. And if you are weak – know your place and be quiet.

The goal of another person appears in the guise of fashion and prestige. Pendulums need to lure you to the life tracks of other people, thus they will be trying their utmost. The carrot must look very appetizing. Then the mind will rush to it without thinking. Pendulums cannot make you follow the rule "do as I do" in all situations. You must want it yourself. The myths about the successful careers of the stars are created to serve that purpose. These myths demonstrate the algorithm of their success and present you with the choice: either to repeat someone else's experience, or to be left with nothing. How could you know how to achieve success? But the stars know – their results are the direct evidence of that. However, as it has already been demonstrated, the stars achieve success just because they break the rule "do as I do" and go their own way. *The algorithm of your success is not known to anyone but your soul.*

The goal of another person is only so tempting because it is so hard to achieve. Man works the following way – everything that is under lock and key is attractive. Inaccessibility gives rise to the desire to possess. Such a property of the human psyche has its origin in childhood, when you want a lot, but only a few things are available to you. It is often the case that if the child has been denied his toy, then he will eat his heart out until he gets it. And then he finally gets the toy, he loses all interest in it. Adults have other toys, but they too behave like children. For example, a grown up child is tone-deaf and has no voice, but he think that he loves to sing. In reality, "the singing bird" doesn't want to come to terms with the fact that it is not his path. After all, others are doing really well at singing, how am I worse? Throw away the importance of the goal and answer the question: do you really want this with all your soul or do you just want to want? *If by reaching the goal you want to prove something to yourself and to everybody else, then it is the wrong goal.* Your goal is not a heavy burden hanging around your neck – your goal simply gives you true pleasure.

The goal of another person is imposed by other people. No one, but yourself can determine your goal. You can calmly listen to the preaching of "those who know" about what you should *do*. Make your own conclusion and do what you feel is right. But as soon as someone is trying to teach you, what you should *strive for*, instantly reject such a rude intrusion into your soul. She has already plenty of wild ideas of her mind. No one can point to your goal. There is, however, one exception – a phrase that has been said accidentally, in passing. As you remember, accidental phrases could be signs. If it is a sign, you will sense it right away. Someone's unpremeditated phrase could suddenly light a small spark in your soul. If your goal has been touched upon, then the soul will liven up, and it will help you realize that it is "what you need". But it has to be a situation, when nobody is trying to convince you or put you on the right path. Instead, it is a situation when, as if incidentally, a person makes some kind of comment or a recommendation to you.

The goal of another person serves to improve the well-being of someone else. If the goal does not improve your life, then it is not your goal. True goals always work for you, for your well-being and success. Your goal is only needed by you. If it *directly* serves to satisfy the needs of others and improving the well-being of others, then it is the goal of another person. Pendulums will try to make you serve other people under any plausible excuse. There are all kinds of different ways of doing this. The words "must", "have to", "ought to" usually have an effect on people with a heightened feeling of guilt. These people really do find comfort in working off their supposed sins. Others might be affected by the slogan "Your help is needed". That works too. As you understand, such methods are maintained by internal and external importance. You cannot make others happy. But you could easily do them harm, if you are unhappy yourself.

The goal of another person evokes feelings of emotional discomfort in your soul. False goals are usually very attractive. The mind will be thrilled to describe all possible virtues of the goal in glowing terms. But if something is putting you down, despite all the attractiveness of the goal, then you have to be honest with yourself. Of course, your mind doesn't want to hear it: everything is great and wonderful. Then where did the shadow of discomfort come from? I am repeating the important rule from the previous chapter: *when thinking about your goal, do not think about how prestigious and unattainable it is, nor should you be thinking about the means of achieving it – pay attention only to the state of emotional comfort of your soul.* Imagine that you've reached the goal and everything is behind. Are you feeling good or are you feeling bad? If there is a sense of fear or a heavy feeling mixed up in your pleasure, then you are sensing the emotional discomfort of your soul. Should you get involved with someone else's goal? Your goal will be even more attractive and will give you even greater pleasure without any discomfort whatsoever. You only need to turn away from the pendulums and find your goal.

If you are not satisfied with the place you are currently occupying in this world or if you are being followed by a chain of unfortunate events, then it means that at some point in your life, you came under the influence of destructive pendulums and started walking towards someone else's goal through someone else's door. The goals of others require a lot of energy and effort. Your goals, on the other hand, are achieved as if on their own. Everything runs along smoothly. The goals and doors of others always doom you to suffering. Find your goal and your door, and then all problems will disappear.

You could say: "And what if I do not know what I want, how do I find out?" I'll ask a counter-question: have you ever seriously thought about what you want? Strangely enough, most people are so busy doing things for pendulums that they are literally burning the candle at both ends and cannot find time for themselves, for their soul. Questions about what they really want out of life are being solved hastily, in passing, in snatches, without thinking about it and while being under pressure of all the problems that exist in their lives. You do not need to do any soul-digging. It is enough to calm down and find a place to be alone, if only for a little while, and nevertheless listen to the rustling of the morning stars.

And what if you do not want anything at all? That shows that your energy potential is extremely low. Being in the state of depression, apathy – is clear evidence of the fact that you only have enough energy to maintain your existence. Then you should increase your energy reserves. It is not possible for your soul to not want anything at all. You just do not have enough power to hear it.

Breaking the Stereotypes

Even though there has already been said a great deal about pendulums, I would like to give a few more examples of how they could lead you astray. Ask yourself the question, is a pendulum imposing someone else's goal on you under some plausible excuse? For example, "a kind soul" is asked for help. The help could be needed by, for example, defenseless animals, wounded soldiers, hungry children or someone else that is in need of care. Or perhaps somewhere people are fighting for their freedom, and they need your courageous heart there. A kind soul will immediately fly over to the place where she is needed.

Yet, it is actually not "a kind soul", but rather "a kind mind" that flies over. Moreover, it is not kind at all, but simply *soulless*. This mind forgot about his soul and rushed off to help the souls of others. It is the same as leaving one's children in trouble, and go away to save others. "The kind mind" drove his soul into a box and remained face to face with his own "sensible" thoughts. *An inner void* was created, and it has to be filled with something.

Pendulums instantly offer all kind of compensations. You'll be shown the widest selection of ways to waste your energy for the benefit of others. Yet, isn't it exactly why a man so keenly answers the calls of others, because he is empty inside? What the common stereotypes pose off as kindness and tenderness, could actually turn out to be the feeling of emptiness in the place where the soul previously resided. The empty place is compensated by caring for others, while the needs of your soul remain unsatisfied. Pendulums benefit from pretending that caring for others is the same as the generosity of the soul.

As you see, pendulums are able to skillfully form the most convincing stereotypes. But that is nothing but beautiful demagoguery. And what about your own soul? Will your mind really forsake her for others? That is why I am so strongly recommending you to turn away from pendulums and let your soul out of the box. Having come to love yourself, you will find your goal. On the way to your goal, you will do plenty of truly good and useful deeds. And, of course, you will help a lot of poor and unfortunate ones, as you will have greater means.

Say, two pendulums are about to make a fight. One declares himself the just liberator and accuses the other of being a dictator and a potentially dangerous aggressor. Actually, the just pendulum simply wants to swallow his rival, to seize his oil or other resources. But that is kept secret, and a large propaganda campaign is being launched promoting freedom and justice.

A man that has been imbued with a sense of importance and swallowed the bait of this pendulum, is telling himself: "I will free the oppressed nation. I'll show that dictator and aggressor!" Meanwhile, another pendulum is forming his camp of adherents. The dictator-pendulum is claiming that he is actually good-hearted, and that he, who declared himself the liberator, is the real aggressor. Another person, full of importance, is boiling with indignation: "Why, they declared war, and didn't ask me?! I'll go outside and fiercely show my protest!" He could even go to war and give his life for someone else's freedom.

As you see, the adherents of the first, as well as of the other camp, are being involved in the battle of pendulums because their internal and external importance is elevated. These adherents are empty inside their souls are locked up in boxes. There is nothing to fill that void of theirs and so it gets bigger instead. After all, what do these adherents gain by getting involved in the battle? The advocates of war try to convince themselves: they were tricked, in reality no one needs this war, and it brings misfortune to all its participants. The advocates of peace too get a flick on the nose. That defenseless nation, which was attacked by the aggressor-pendulum, is quick to reject its beaten ruler and is already raiding the consulate of the country-protector of peace, stealing its humanitarian aid, while starting to grovel before the aggressor.

It is absolutely obvious that all the high ideals, which the adherents hold in the battle of pendulums, are like soap bubbles. There is emptiness inside, but on the surface – a rainbow coating made out of inflated importance. Do the souls of the adherents really need all this fuss?

When the goal that has been determined by you is not serving you personally, but others instead – you could test whether it is yours or not it by using this simple method. *If the care for others is imposed on you from the outside, no matter in what way, then it is someone else's goal.* If, however, caring for others comes from the inside, from the depths of your soul, then that goal could be yours. For example: "I just love spending time with my pets. It is not a burden to me." Or: "I love my children (grandchildren), and I like taking care of them, watching them grow and rejoicing together with them." Yet, when they grow up, you'll have to look for another goal.

No one, except yourself, is able to identify your goal. There is only one way to find your goal: to drop importance, turn away from pendulums and face your soul. To, first of all, love and care about yourself. Only then could you find the way to your goal.

The mistake of the mind is also that he immediately tries to evaluate how realistic it is to achieve the goal and to calculate all ways and means in advance. Because everything has to be rational. If it is not very likely that the goal could be realistically achieved, then it is basically being rejected, or put off. With an attitude like that, a man will never manage to tune into the life track of his goal. On the contrary, *thinking about the means of achieving the goal, the man is tuning into the track of failure.* He is, after all, playing all possible scenarios of defeat in his head. The goal won't be achieved by common means, and there won't be a miracle. Indeed, the hard to achieve objective is rarely realized within the framework of the usual worldview. And it really should be that way, because the parameters of those who doubt don't in any way correspond to the track of their goal.

A miracle will happen only if you were to break the common stereotype and start thinking about the actual goal, and not about the

means of achieving it. Then, what previously seemed unlikely will
no longer appear as such. Suddenly, as if incidentally, a quite real
way of achieving the goal will be revealed to you. From the
common worldview it will look like a miraculous coincidence. In
that case, the mind can only be at a loss: "Who could have
known?"

From the point of view of Transurfing there is no miracle. You
simply tuned into the frequency of the life track of your goal,
you've got the determination to have, and external intention transferred you onto that life track. And on that life track, new opportunities emerge and doors are opened that you couldn't even think
of on your former life track.

We are so used to the settled stereotypes that we recognize
them as valuable experience that has been gained by humankind.
In reality, stereotypes are formed by pendulums, and people are
made to agree with them. The entire society is based on
pendulums that live and develop on their own, according to their
own laws, as energy informational beings that have submitted
adherents to their will. The influence of pendulums on man is so
great that his mind literally becomes clouded and loses the ability
to reason independently and consciously.

Take, for example, the crimes of German Nazis during Second
World War. They were doing terrible things. Perhaps, the Nazis
were very cruel people with pathological sadistic tendencies? No,
most of them were just as normal as you and I. They had families;
they loved them and cared for them as well. Having returned from
the war, they entered the peaceful life and became your regular
good-natured townsmen.

Why then does a respectable family man turn into an animal,
when he is at war? That happens because his mind gets in the
power of a pendulum. The adherents, involved in the battle of
pendulums, are literally unaware of what they are doing. This
becomes especially obvious in the sometimes pointless and cruel
behavior of teenagers. The young and unstable psyche is especially
defenseless and subject to influence. Take each of these teenagers
on their own. Is any one of them cruel? Not at all, and their parents

will swear on that. But, having come under the influence of a pendulum, for example, having become part of the crowd, a teenage boy or girl will stop being conscious of his or her actions. The mind of a member of the crowd is literally asleep, because it is caught in the noose of the pendulum. Remember the mechanism of induced transfer?

All evil, cruelty and violence in this world does not origin from the supposed low nature of humankind, but from the greedy nature of pendulums. The soul of man knows no evil. All evil is concentrated in his mind as a layer left over from the destructive influence of pendulums.

Pendulums provoke people into taking to violence not only in regards to other people, but also to themselves. How do you like the following brave slogan: "Nothing risked, nothing gained"? It contains a provocation, a call to put one's well-being or life at stake in the name of someone else's idea. Of course, if it is your idea, and not someone else's and the risk is thus justified, then perhaps it is worth risking. Yet, there is nothing more foolish than an unjustified risk, putting your health and life in jeopardy.

Pendulums provoke man to take risky actions, because fear, tension and excitement experienced by the person taking the risk - are the most favorite energy dishes of pendulums. A pendulum tries to hook its victim, using the stereotype of false courage or with the help of a specific adherent: "Come on, be a man! Show us what you are made of! You don't want to look like a coward now, do you?" And the man, filled with internal importance, rushes off to prove the opposite, to himself and everyone else. He is in a trap of a false stereotype, and it doesn't occur to him that he doesn't have to prove anything to anybody, and that he can go ahead and not give a damn about what pendulums think.

The feeling of personal inadequacy forces the man to be on the pendulums' leash. Obviously, an unjustified risk – is not at all a demonstration of one's courage, but rather an attempt to hide one's false complexes. The mind is irresponsibly managing the life of his soul in favor of dubious stereotypes. The poor little soul, having shrunk into a tiny lump, is watching with terror what the unbridled mind is up to, but she is unable to do anything about it. The mind is acting towards the soul as a chronic loser at best, and at worst – as a drunk and angry brute that is beating his defenseless child.

Let your mind wake up from this nightmare. He has in his possession a priceless and wonderful treasure – his soul. Having united your soul and mind, you will gain true freedom and power. Do not be afraid to break the stereotypes that have been formed by pendulums. The true nature of many things in this world will be revealed to you. *By breaking the stereotypes, you are opening forbidden doors.*

Your Goals

I assume from the very beginning that you have a secret wish and that you have at least some idea of how it could be made true. Even if you do not have any idea about how your wish could be realized, it is not the end of the world. If you will have the determination to have, there will be an option for you. The most important thing is – to determine a truly innermost wish of yours and to obtain the determination to have and act. Intention turns a wish into a goal. A wish without intention will never come true. But first, you need to make it clear to yourself what you actually want out of this life. Diffuse phrasings like "I want to be rich and happy" won't work.

Imagine that you are walking downtown without any particular goal. You are just aimlessly wandering about. Where will you end up? No one knows. If there is, however, a specific destination, then sooner or later you will get there, even if you do not know the specifics of the route. Same thing in life: if you don't have a goal, then you are a little paper boat on stormy waters. If there is a goal and you are striving towards it, you could very well reach it. Or not.

There is only one case, when it can be one hundred percent guaranteed that you will reach your goal: if the goal is yours and you are walking towards it through your door. In that case, no one and nothing could stop you, because the fraile key of your soul is an ideal match to the lock of your path, your door. No one can take what's yours. So there won't be any problems reaching the goal. It is only a problem finding your goal and your door.

First of all, the goal is not determined by any temporary needs. It should answer the question: *what do you want out of life? What will make your life an enjoyable and happy one?* Only that matters. You could consider everything else to be pendulum leftovers.

Find your one main goal. *Reaching that goal will lead to the fulfillment of all your other desires.* If you cannot think of something specific, then you could, for example, phrase the following general goal for a start: you want comfort and well-being out of life. What is comfort and well-being to you? The need to have a house, a car, nice clothes and other attributes of a comfortable life could be replaced with one goal – to get a high-paid job. But, as you understand, that is not even *a goal,* but *a door* and an ambiguous one at that.

The high-paid job could be replaced with an even more specific formulation – to become a very good or unique specialist in your area. *What is your soul into?* Yet, a question arises: will that job fill the entire meaning of your life? If that is the case, then you are in luck – your goal matches your door. Let's assume that your soul is into a specific area of science, culture or art. Then by doing what you love to do, you will be making discoveries and creating masterpieces. Happiness on such a life track is something that is here and now, and not somewhere ahead you. All attributes of a comfortable life that others get by doing such hard work, will come on their own, as something that goes without saying. After all, you are walking on your path.

However, if what you like to do, even if it is your favorite thing to do, is not that *one and only thing,* which will bring you joy and fill your entire life with attributes of comfort, then that thing could perhaps be considered a door, but it could never be called a goal. Do not forget that your goal must turn your life into a celebration with all associated attributes. Don't be thinking about the means of achieving the goal just yet – that is don't be thinking about doors that lead to your goal. The main thing – is to identify the goal. The doors will turn up on their own in due time.

Ask yourself the question: *what is your soul into? What will turn your life into a celebration?* Drop any thoughts you may have about how prestigious and hard to achieve your supposed goal is. You should not be interested in any limitations. If you do not believe, then at least pretend that everything is available to you, and you only have to choose. Don't be shy and order to the fullest.

You wanted to have a boat? How about your own yacht?

You wanted to have a flat? How about your own mansion?

You wanted to be the head of department? How about the position of the CEO?

You wanted to work a lot in order to get a lot of money? How about not working all together and living for your own pleasure?

You wanted to buy some inexpensive land in order to build a house? How about your own island in the Mediterranean Sea?

You could carry on with these "Then how about..." forever. You can't even imagine how modest your requests are in comparison to what you could get, if you were to walk towards your goal through your door.

Do not make your wish with your mind. Allow yourself plenty of time to find out what your soul wants. The expression "it's to my (soul's) liking" speaks for itself. It doesn't reflect an opinion, but rather an attitude. Opinion – is a product of your mind's cognitive activity. An attitude stems from the depths of your soul. Thus, only an attitude could function as a determinant of your own goals and the goals of others. When you are in the process of identifying your goal, you should keep asking yourself: "How do I feel in the context of the achieved goal?"

Let's say you've made a wish. In order to see whether it is truly your wish or not, ask yourself two questions. The first one: do I really need this? Second: but do I really need this after all? Try all of the characteristics of someone else's goal onto that wish.

Do you really want it with your whole soul or do you just *want to want it?* Are you trying to prove something to yourself and others? Do you really want it? Perhaps it is a fashion or prestige tribute? A disabled person may believe that he wants to ice-skate with his whole heart. But in reality, such a goal does not come from the heart, but from the feelings of resentment for his inadequacy. The goal tempts him with being so unachievable. If the goal is accessible, try to reject it and keep an eye out for your reaction. If you felt a relief, then it is someone else's goal. If you feel upset and there is an inner protest, then the goal could be yours.

The one and only reliable criterion in choosing your goal is the emotional discomfort of your soul. *This is a negative reaction of your soul to a decision that has already been made by your mind.* The state of emotional comfort could be tested only once the mind has made a decision and has identified his goal. Imagine that you've attained the goal and it is now all behind. As soon as you've done that, you should stop discussing the goal and listen closely to the feelings of your soul. Do you feel good or not? If you experience mixed feelings of joy and fear, or a heavy and burdening feeling, or a feeling of necessity, a sense of obligation of some sort, then your soul is clearly saying "no". The mind could not even conjecture what kind of troubles that goal has in its pocket, even though it is so nicely wrapped. But the soul, however, does feel the true nature of the goal.

The feelings of emotional discomfort could be vague and indistinct. Do not confuse your soul feeling constraint with her experiencing emotional discomfort. As it was already mentioned in the previous chapter, constraint or some kind of timidity is a result of an unusual situation that your soul finds herself in: "Is all of this for me? Really?" *Emotional discomfort of your soul – is a heavy or burdening feeling, which appears vague in comparison to the optimistic argumentations of your mind in the background.* The constraint of your soul could be eliminated with the help of the slides, the emotional discomfort of your soul, however, can never be eliminated. It would be the biggest mistake to think that you are not worthy of something that you want. Total nonsense! Pendulums made you put such a primitive label on yourself. You are worthy of all the best. In any case, do not be in a hurry to make a final decision. Try to experience your goal by using the slides. If you notice that the oppressing feeling is not diminishing with time, then you are dealing with a discomfort of your soul.

If you experience a discomfort in your soul in relation to specific aspects of the actual goal, then it is someone else's goal. If you experience discomfort from the idea that the goal is hard to achieve, then the goal is not part of your comfort zone, or you have chosen someone else's door. *Do not think about the means of achieving the goal, until you have clearly identified your goal.* If you cannot manage to get a clear picture of yourself in the planned role, perhaps you are not ready to accept it just yet. The comfort zone could be expanded by using slides. Do not worry about the doors. The determination to have is the only thing required of you. Then external intention will sooner or later point out the right door.

Do not fall for the temptation to identify money as your goal. As if saying that once I have money, then all my problems will be solved. I know what to buy for that money. Remember the briefcase, packed with dollar bills, in the chapter "Slides"? It is said there that money can not be a goal. It is only an attribute. You could immediately agree with this opinion, nonetheless, it is not an entirely trivial statement. We are all so used to money that we could put a price tag on almost everything. But money – is an abstract category that is intended for the mind, but not in any way for the soul. The soul has no idea about what to do with money, because she is unable to think in abstract terms. The end goal must be clear to your soul. She has to know what you want to buy for the money you requested: a house, a casino, an island and so on. There is no talk of means, as long as your soul likes it.

As long as your inner accounts department will keep calculating the means of achieving the goal, you won't be able to identify your goal and tune into the life track of your goal. Activate your Watcher and pull yourself up every time your mind is trying to avoid answering the following question: "What do I want out of life?" The stereotype of a goal being hard to achieve – is the most persistent of them all, so you will need some patience. Your mind will keep trying to answer another question: "How to achieve this?" That is when your soul should tell your mind: "Be quiet, it is not your concern, we are choosing a toy!"

You must strive to be free from destructive pendulums, but it doesn't mean that you have to isolate yourself all together. The entire society is built upon pendulum interaction, so you would have to either leave for the Himalayas, or to look for pendulums of your own. It is easy for hermits to "speak with the Universe", as they are far away from pendulums. But should you only get one of these hermits back into the aggressive environment of pendulums, as he will instantly lose his balance and any sense of detachment.

Your goal too belongs to a pendulum. There is no danger for you in that, as long as your goal is true. Find your goal, and the pendulum will be forced to make you his favorite. You could even create a new pendulum. The important ting is – to realize your right to have the freedom of choice and not to let pendulums establish control over you.

You won't be able to identify your goal by means of analysis and reasoning. Only your soul is capable of identifying the true goal. Analysis – is the activity of your mind. Your soul is unable to reason. She is only able to see and feel.

The task of your mind is not to look for a goal in the process of looking for a goal. Your mind will do it the usual way that is by using analytical methods and by constructing logical arguments based on commonly accepted stereotypes and labels. If one could determine one's entire life path this way, then everyone would be happy.

The task of your mind is to process all of the external information, paying particular attention to the emotional comfort of your soul. Your mind needs only to have one aim: I am looking for something that will turn my life into a celebration. And then he can let external information in and keep an eye on the feelings of the soul, having the above aim in mind.

An active search for your path will get you nowhere. Do not worry. Just keep waiting and watching. If you'll have the search for your goal as your aim, then the needed information will come on its own. At some specific point, you'll get a piece of information that will spark a live interest in you. The main thing is to make sure that your mind is not getting in the way with his thoughts in that very moment. He should instead be paying attention to the emotional state of your soul.

You could speed up the arrival of the needed information. A most useful thing to do is to get more interests. Venture out, go where you haven't been yet: to a museum, on a guided tour, to the movies, on a camping trip, to another part of your town, to a book shop, where ever. You do not need to be actively out there – searching. Simply expand the range of external information and watch.

Give yourself unlimited amount of time. Do not squeeze yourself into a time frame and do not turn the search for your goal into something that you have to do. Just keep in mind the following aim: *I am looking for something that will turn my life into a celebration.*

Keep an eye on your feelings and be more attentive to them than you were before. Let this aim of yours always be present and active in the background. Put any received information through the questioning filter: how do I feel about that? Do I like it or not?

Sooner or later you will get some kind of sign or information that will light a spark in you: "Oh, I like that!" You should thoroughly consider the information you have received from all possible angles, carefully observing the emotional state of your soul.

But let's say, you finally managed to get rid of the temptation to think about the means, and you have identified your goal. Once you have the determination to have and to act in the name of this goal, then the layer of your world will undergo an amazing transformation. And this is what will happen.

You have freed yourself from the burden of false goals and you are breathing again. You no longer have the need to make yourself do what your soul doesn't want to do. You have abandoned the struggle for illusory happiness in the future, and you allowed yourself to be happy right here and now. Before, you were trying to fill the empty space in your soul with cheap surrogates, offered to you by pendulums. But now, your mind has let your soul out of the box, and you experience a feeling of ease and freedom, as if

Spring has arrived, and you have woken up from a long Winter hibernation sleep. The heavy and burdening feeling of oppression has disappeared. Wouldn't you agree that it is much more pleasant to move towards your own goal, knowing that you have found inside yourself something that you have previously and unsuccessfully tried to find in the outside world? Your mind has thrown away the unnecessary garbage of someone else's goals and simply allowed the right objective into the layer of his world. The soul chose her toy herself and started jumping around and clapping her hands out of joy. You have forced open the false stereotype and allowed yourself to have, despite the supposed inaccessibility of your goal. Thus, doors that were closed to you in the past are now standing open before you. At this point, your mind finally realized as well that the goal could really be achieved. Now your life will turn into a celebration, because your happy soul will skip along, following your mind that let the goal into the layer of his world. Your soul and mind will start walking happily, hand in hand, along the even and pleasant path to happiness that is already here and now.

Your Doors
If you constantly have to overcome obstacles on the way to your goal, then either you have chosen someone else's goal, or you are walking toward your goal through someone else's door. The only thing in life that could be considered important - is identifying your goal and door. Striving towards the goals of others, you could waste your entire life and not get anywhere. There is nothing sadder than admitting to the fact that all your efforts have been in vain and that your life is a failure.

Pendulums have trained people to do what is necessary, and to accept it as the matter of course. The stereotype of *forced necessity* is carried to the point of absurdity: as if life – is a sentence that everyone has to serve, or a civil service that everyone has to work off. Man gets so used to the sense of necessity that the true tendencies of his soul are put away in the darkest corner of his consciousness, to await better times. But life ends, yet better times never come.

Happiness is always somewhere in the future. The false stereotype claims that: in order for the future to arrive, you have to win, earn or achieve it. People often abandon their favorite hobby because of financial reasons. Activities are divided into interests and work that has to generate an income. Along with the arrangement of false goals, forced necessity is yet another method used by pendulums in their attempts to lure a person as far away from his path as possible.

In reality, you could make good money even by dedicating yourself to your hobby, if it is your goal, of course. If you are forced to abandon your favorite hobby just because it doesn't generate an income, then you need to make sure that this hobby is somehow related to the goal that has been chosen by your soul. Will your favorite hobby turn your life into a celebration or not? If that hobby cannot be ascribed to your goal, then one could not say for sure whether it will generate an income or not. But if you are certain that your hobby is that very thing; expect the attributes of comfort to make an appearance in your life. When the goal matches the door, a person doesn't have to worry about financial well-being. He will have everything anyway, if he would want it.

However, the false stereotype of forced necessity doesn't allow a person to dedicate himself to his goal completely. There are plenty of examples supporting this claim. There is this odd fellow, he is going to his necessary work just like everyone else, and in his spare time he is creating or inventing things. It doesn't even occur to him that his creations could be sold for a lot of money. He lives in poverty, absolutely convinced that he has to work hard for a little piece of bread. While his interest – is just something he does, "for the good of his soul". See, what's happening here? The man is working for some guy for the most part of his life – thinking that it is essential for his existence. While his soul is getting crumbs left over from the main working time. So for whom does this man live? For that guy?

If your goal matches your door, you will make a fortune with your hobby. Having achieved your goal will attract the fulfillment of all your other desires, and what's more, *the results will exceed all expectations*. Have no doubt; everything in this world that was made by a soul is very expensive. The products of pure mind are, in contrast, not worth a lot. As you know, true masterpieces are created by the unity of soul and mind. On the way to your goal, you will create masterpieces, unless you'll let pendulums side-track you. In that case everything is rather simple: you only have to calmly follow your path and avoid falling for any of their tricks. Sooner or later you will achieve grand success.

It is a bit trickier if your goal and door do not happen to match. Although, before arriving at this conclusion, think about it very carefully. Your goal cannot make your life much more difficult. On the contrary, having chosen your goal, you will make your life considerably easier and you'll also get rid of a lot of problems. Do not be in a rush to choose your door. If you have the determination to have, the door will turn up. If you do not have a clear idea about the location of your door, then keep working with the slides and keep expanding your comfort zone. Drop importance and abandon the desire to reach the goal. As soon as you *allow yourself to have*, external intention will present you with a suitable option.

Your door is the path that will lead you to your goal. Once you have identified your goal, ask yourself the question: how could this goal be achieved? External intention will sooner or later reveal the various options. Your task is to find your door among these. Examine all possible options. Each option must be tested for the state of emotional comfort of your soul. At this point you could follow the same principles that were used when you were choosing your goal.

Let's assume that your goal implies that you are rich. Then you have to determine, how you are going to get rich. After all, money doesn't simply come to a man, but to what he is. It could be: a show biz star, a large industrialist, an investor, an outstanding specialist, or an heir. So who would you like to be? You need to find your very own path to the wealth – something that your heart is into. You must ask your soul, and not your mind, what your heart is into. Your mind is a product of society. And society is based on pendulums. Society says: "Become a celebrity, a politician, a wealthy man – it is prestigious." But since your personal happiness is of no interest to the pendulum, he will not aid you in determining the right niche in this life.

Your mind and people you know tell you that you need to look for a high-paid job, for example that of a lawyer. Everyone is saying: having become a qualified lawyer, you will earn loads of money. Of course, you really want to make a lot of money, but that door could turn out to be someone else's door. That door might take you somewhere completely different. If the goal was chosen correctly, then the door will reveal opportunities you could never even dream of. Let's say that you want the following out of life – to have your own house, a car, a good salary. When you enter through your door, you will get so much that your former requests will simply look ridiculous. But for that to happen you need to make the right choice when it comes to your door.

Do not be in a rush and give yourself plenty of time to make the choice. You will waste much more time and effort if you hurry and make the wrong choice. *It could take months to determine one's goals and doors.* During that time, you would need to keep a kind of "impeccability fast" – where possible, you should undeviatingly follow the main principles of Transurfing. You are already familiar with them.

First of all – awareness. You should be aware of the motives of any subsequent actions on your part. Are you acting consciously? Do you understand and are you aware of the rules of the game? Or are you obeying a pendulum, with little will of your own?

Keep an eye on the levels of your internal and external importance. Think about your goal and door as if you already have it. There is no prestige, inaccessibility and necessity. Remove any importance. What you possess is something that is ordinary to you.

Accept in advance any possible failure. If things work out – great, if not – then the goal was not yours to begin with, so there is nothing to be sad about. Allow yourself to make mistakes. Make some room for a defeat in your life. Let it be under your supervision. Moreover, further in the book you will find out that a disappointing failure is not a defeat at all; rather it is just another milestone on your way to your goal.

Find a safety net for that particular goal – a replacement. Do not abandon your former door right away. Do not burn the bridges behind you – proceed with caution. Do not put all your eggs in one basket. Have other alternatives available.

Do not stop playing the slide of your goal in your mind. By doing that, you are expanding your comfort zone and you are also tuning yourself into the frequency of your goal's life track. External intention will provide you with the information you need.

In order not to miss that information, *you should put the slide of looking for* your *goal and door into your head.* Let all the information from the outside world pass through this slide. Assess whether any of it suits you or not. Keep listening to the rustling of the morning stars, and not to what your mind is saying. *Meanwhile, you should keep an eye on what is putting you down or makes you fly, and not what you think about that piece of information.* Pay attention to the attitude of your soul to any information. At some point she will liven up and exclaim: "This is exactly what I need!"

And again, do not be in a hurry. Keep expanding your comfort zone and set your thoughts on the life track of your goal until your goal and door take on a clear shape. You should come to a distinct conclusion: "Yes, I want this, and it will turn my life into a celebration". Your soul is singing, while your mind is rubbing his hands with satisfaction.

If your soul is already singing, but your mind is still in doubt, keep expanding your comfort zone. That will allow you to break the interfering false stereotype of your goal being unattainable and unrealistic. Do you know why a door appears to be inaccessible? It is because it is barred with the false stereotype of inaccessibility, sitting in your mind. Once you'll force the stereotype, the door will open.

I am not urging you to believe me, or yourself, or anyone else. You will never make your mind believe. Your mind accepts only facts without any reserve. So, in order to make the door appear real to your mind, you need to transfer to the life track of your goal.

And that can only be done with the help of a slide containing your goal. At the beginning of your life track, the goal is still ahead, but the ways of achieving it are already real and clearly visible. *Trying to convince yourself and fighting the stereotype is pointless.* Forcing the stereotype is not about that. *The stereotype will collapse on its own, when external intention will show you new opportunities on the life track of your goal.* That is why I am drawing your attention to the following: do not attempt to convince yourself and do not fight the stereotype. *Everything you need - is to systematically keep playing the slide of your goal in your mind.* These are not empty and speculative exercises, but a specific movement towards the goal.

Do not forget that material realization is inert and hence, external intention cannot carry out your order right away. You will have to be patient. And if you are not patient enough, then you passionately want to achieve your goal as soon as possible. If that is the case, then start over and keep lowering importance. If you desire, then you have doubts about whether your goal could really be achieved. Again, keep expanding your zone of comfort until you see that real perspectives are opening before you.

Pendulums could mask your door with a cover of false insignificance and low value. *Everything that you are able to do easily, naturally and with pleasure - has significance and value.* You do not have one single virtue that is insignificant. Any foolishness that is characteristic of you, but is of no value within the stereotype frame, could be the key to the right door. Try to project the "unserious" quality that is characteristic of you onto some serious doors.

For example, if you have the reputation of being "a clown", then perhaps you would become a great comedian. If everyone is saying that you are completely useless, the only thing you can do is to dress up and gussy up - perhaps your door leads to the profession of a top-model, make up artist or a designer. If you are annoyed by advertisement and you like grumbling about that it is being done the wrong way, and that it should be presented in a completely different way - then it is not simply your dissatisfaction talking, but a hidden desire to develop your talents in this particular area. I have listed particular examples. A personal "useless" quality could be manifested in a rather unforeseen way. That way will reveal itself to you, if you turn away from pendulums to face your soul. Think about it: if you are actually making your silly actions naturally and with pleasure, then it must have some kind of significance.

Everything mentioned above has to do with the process of choosing one's door. But let's say you are already on your way to the chosen goal. Then there is one way to find out whether the door you chose is the right one for you. If you are losing your energy and are getting tired and exhausted on your way to your goal, then it is not your door. In contrast, *if you are caught up by inspiration, when you are doing something that is getting you closer to your goal, then you could go ahead and consider that something your door.*

There is one more way you could tell that it is the right door for you. Someone else's door could pretend to be yours; you can almost feel it being opened before you, but at the most crucial moment it is slammed in your face. Turns out that on your way through someone else's door it is as if everything is ok, but in the end, when it really matters, everything flops. If things like that have happened to you before, then you were walking through someone else's door. Such is the quality of pendulums, which are opening *doors that are available to all* on purpose, so as to lure as many adherents as possible to walk through that door.

Usually, there is no crowd before your door. But even if you have met a lot of people, wanting to walk through your door, everyone will instantly make way for you, and you will have free passage. Doors that are available to all are open for all, but only a few walk through them. Recall once again, how pendulums are creating myths of a star's successful career and how they are trying to make everyone follow the rule "do as I do". People that are carried away with the mirage are all forcing one and the same door together, while their own doors are standing nearby and are completely open.

However, even your door could be closed before you. That

happens if you have heavily violated the law of balance. For example, if the goal is of too great of importance to you and you are ready to risk everything in order to achieve it. This door could be opened again, if you were to lower its significance. We will talk about that in the end of this chapter.

Intention
I think that if you have spent time identifying your goal and door, then you have intention. *Intention turns a desire into a goal.* A desire without intention will never be fulfilled. Dreams do not come true either. What is the difference between a goal and a dream? The difference is the same as between intention and desire. If you have intention, your dream is transformed into a goal. Empty dreams and castles in the sky can't change anything. Only intention, which is the determination to have and act, is capable of changing your life.

Let's assume that you have managed to identify your goal, and you are fully determined to achieve it. You are all agog to start acting as soon as possible. Now – loosen your grip. Drop the importance of the goal, abandon the desire to achieve it and leave only the determination to have. The only thing left for you to do is to act within the limits of purified intention, that is, to do everything that is required of you *without wanting or insisting.*

The only thing that could ruin everything on your way to your goal - is any excessive responsibility, diligence, meticulousness and compulsion on your part. It does sound strange and unusual, if you were to consider it within the limits of the common worldview. But I hope that you now do not find anything absurd about that. Let's put everything back on its feet.

There is no need to make any extra effort when you are moving towards your goal through your door. You won't have to force yourself either. If that is not that case, then you've got someone else's goal or door. However, your mind is used to struggling and overcoming obstacles. The mind is creating all his problems himself, when he starts attributing excessive significance to things and starts fighting the flow of variations. Your life track has a minimum of obstacles, if you lay off importance.

You must walk towards your goal, as if you are going to get your mail from the mailbox. What is then left of intention, if it has been cleaned of importance and the desire to reach the goal? There is only the determination to have and the determination to move your feet. Stop thinking about the mail in your mailbox as a problem, and simply start moving your feet in its direction. Do not be thinking about the problem – act, any way you can, and the problem will be solved in the process of moving towards your goal.

Internal intention of your mind prompts you to beat the water with your hands: "I insist that…" External intention works in a completely different way: "Turns out that…" *As long as you are insisting, you are not letting external intention realize your goal along the flow of variations.* How could your mind know exactly how your goal should be realized?

Moving towards the right goal through your door is a smooth process. No one and nothing is bothering you, that is if your importance is on a minimum level and you are not fighting the flow of variations. Since you are following your path, there is nothing to worry about, even if some temporary difficulties may arise. Let yourself enjoy life and accept everything as gifts. As soon as your celebration is clouded by something, try to determine *where you elevated the level of importance.* Why do you feel heavy at heart? There is a standard answer to this question: you are forcing yourself too much, or you cannot wait to achieve the goal, or you are attributing excessive significance to something. Loosen your grip.

Depressing thoughts and feelings could appear because your comfort zone is not wide enough. Let's say that as a result of reaching the goal you should get a large amount of money. Instantly, there is a whole array of worrying thoughts: where should I keep the money? What is the best investment to make? What if I lose it? How do I best spend it? And what if someone takes it from me? If all these thoughts pop into your head, then you are not ready to have it. When the realization of your dream is associated with problems of this kind, then as a result your soul would unavoidably feel constraint and thus, on the subconscious level, you will strive towards relieving yourself of these problems. In that case, external intention will be working against you.

The determination to have must be maintained at all times. And you won't have to make yourself play the slide of your goal in your mind. After all, you like thinking about your desired goal. Just don't try to persuade or convince yourself. You could be persuading yourself for a very long time and it would be completely pointless. Intention, in contrast to auto-suggestion, implies that a decision has been made and it is not subject to discussion. It is obvious that the goal will be achieved. *Any doubts that you may have will disappear, if you will keep expanding your comfort zone.*

I want to caution you against making a gross error. There is one more false stereotype that calls for you to only think about the successful development of events. As strange as it may sound, it is actually a false stereotype. See, how many there are! What do you think; will you manage to only think about success? Hardly. If you will strive to keep all the negative alternatives out of your scenario, then it won't work. You won't manage to convince your mind that everything will go smoothly. Your mind could pretend that he believed it. But deep down in your soul you will still have doubts, because your mind is in doubt. Your soul will definitely find a negative alternative in the basement, where the mind left it.

You do not have to add any scenarios of goal achievement to the slide of your goal. This given slide should only contain the final image of the achieved goal. You already have that. Everything that is required of you is to enjoy the slide and to move your feet with the help of your purified internal intention. Visualizing the process – is you already working with the scenario, but in a completely different key. You are convincing your mind that everything *will not run, but is running* smoothly. Visualizing the current link of the transfer chain is in tune with what you are doing now, and only a step ahead. But trying to convince yourself that it will end with success, you are keeping yourself in a death grip. Loosen the grip, do not think about problems that are not yet present, and keep calmly moving along the flow of variations.

Realization

I was walking on wet pavement...

It's been raining in the morning, and earth worms have crawled out of the lawn onto the pavement, looking for the meaning of life and new discoveries. They all had different destinies. The lucky ones managed to crawl over to the near lying flowerbed with rich black earth. Someone was pecked by the birds. Yet another worm was crushed by the soles of some horrible monster, tramping down the pavement. The sun had warmed the pavement and dried off all of the moisture, catching a worm halfway across the road. He realized his mistake all too late. Now there won't be enough power to crawl over to the other side. A slow and painful death will be standing over that worm for a long time to come, until he dries up completely. And then suddenly, some inconceivable power grabbed the worm and threw him onto the moist earth. Something like that was impossible, from the point of view of the worm. He was unable to grasp it or explain it. But there was nothing supernatural about it to me: I simply felt sorry for the worm, and threw him onto the flowerbed. Apparently, this lonesome Wanderer chose his goal and his door correctly after all.

If your goal appears to be hard to achieve in your eyes, then your entire celebration will be ruined by doubts and heavy thoughts about a possible failure. How should one believe in the impossible, in order to make it possible? That's an example of a silly question. There is no way to believe in the impossible! I once again return to what has already been said. *You will never be able to convince yourself, or persuade yourself, or make yourself believe.* Save yourself this empty trouble and get busy moving your feet on the way to the goal.

The fact that the goal appears to be hard to achieve, should not bother you. It is hard for you to imagine how such a thing could happen. But you are wasting your time worrying about that. Your task is – to choose the order correctly, leave everything else to the waiter. Many people, having achieved breath-taking success, said later: they would never have believed that they would be capable of achieving such results.

The fact that your soul is striving towards the goal, while your mind is worried about the means of achieving the goal, is in the way of the mutual understanding of your soul and mind. Your soul has no idea about the ways of reaching the goal. In your dreams, she is used to getting everything she wants, just like that. Any rush of the soul is instantly realized by the intention of the dream. No one knows where your soul is, while your mind is sleeping. We can only remember the dreams we had, when our mind was dozing. Waking up from a heavy dream, your mind starts setting the sail of the soul in accordance with his expectations and feelings. For that reason, dreams cannot indicate your soul's desires.

For the same reason, we are unable to remember the past lives of our soul, if there were any at all. The mind, in contrast to the soul, enters this world as a blank piece of paper. There are many testimonies of how, under certain circumstances, somebody's mind got access to some information from his former lives. However, that is a different question all together, and it is outside the scope of this particular book.

The mind is forced to think about means, because he is used to act within the limits of internal intention. And there is always a scenario with a sad ending within these limits. Not only will external intention not provide you any help, but it will also act to your disadvantage. That is why I strongly recommend that you stop any thoughts you might have about how events may develop. The determination to have must dominate on your way to your goal – and that is the most important thing that should be on your mind. The remaining part of intention – the determination to have – should be maximally free of desire and importance.

The determination to move your feet – is a dispassionate intention to do a minimum of what is required of you. To act dispassionately does not mean to act apprehensively and without spirit. I think you understand what I am trying to say. Being overly decisive is also a consequence of importance. The more you will be able to free your internal intention of desire and importance, the more efficiently you will act.

You only need to think through the scenario of achieving the goal in general terms: define the main stages on your way to your goal, that is, the links of the transfer chain. It is necessary to stop thinking about the general scenario after that. There should only be the slide of your goal in your mind. This slide contains only the image of the achieved goal and does not include any scenarios. Play the slide in your head at all times, live in it. Your comfort zone will start expanding, and the parameters of your radiation will start tuning into the life track of your goal.

Exclude any manifestations of desire and importance from your attitude, concerning anything that has to do with achieving your goal. If you attempt to strain every nerve to achieve the goal as soon as possible, if you have doubts about your potential, if you fear difficulties, then the level of importance is too high. Allow yourself to be flawed and to make mistakes. If you won't let yourself make mistakes, then others will definitely not let you make them. If you fear that the goal won't be achieved, then it means that you desire. And how not to? Accept failure in advance. Come up with alternative ways and back-up plans. Have them ready. Not having done that, you won't be able to free yourself from desire.

The main thing is – *under no circumstances should you put your goal on the line.* For example, you cannot just leave everything and get carried away with your passions in life. And what if it will soon turn out that you made a mistake and took someone else's goal or door to be your own? And then, by putting all your eggs in one basket, you will upset the balance. There has always got to be a plan B, an escape route. Your soul will be calm, and the balancing forces won't harm you. For example, do not leave your job, until you've definitely found a new one. Do not shut the former door. Do not burn your bridges. Be very careful and calculating. Even if you are absolutely sure that the goal and door are yours, never make any sudden movements that will, in the case of failure, leave you starving and homeless. No one is safe from misfortunes.

In any case, you are armed with the powerful Transurfing technique, so there will be much less reasons to worry. At least now you know the rules of the game, and that is already quite a lot. In the world of pendulums, man enters a game with pendulums, without knowing the rules. That is why he is instantly defeated. The methods that you have become familiarized with, give you a great advantage. But that is far from it. In the upcoming chapters you shall find out about "the heavy artillery" of Transurfing.

If you won't interfere with external intention, by doing things that are based on a too high level of importance, then external intention will definitely get you to your goal. Move along the flow of variations and do not try to fight it. The thing that could prompt you to fight the flow is your mind's habit to keep everything under control. But wouldn't you agree that no one can know all the moves in advance. If you are visualizing the slide of your goal, then you are being led by external intention. And it acts outside the frame of the usual scenarios and stereotypes, thus it introduces unexpected changes into the course of the events.

Your mind considers these events as unfortunate, starts beating the water with his hands and ruins everything. In order for that not to happen, allow the scenario to develop dynamically. Release your control, your grip on the situation. If something doesn't work out exactly the way you planned, do not be in a rush to change the situation, try instead to view the unexpected event in a positive light, as something that works in your favor. It is not always obvious at first, but in the majority of cases that is exactly the case. Man gets upset all for nothing, when things are actually not that bad.

I do not call for you to blindly believe the saying "It's all for the best". There are two pieces of truth in this saying: one apparent and one hidden. The apparent bit belongs to common stereotypes and assumes that things are *generally* not that bad. It is true, the flow of variations always moves along the path of least resistance. Trouble always requires large energy expenses, and these are exactly due to the fact that man tries to fight the flow. Changes in the direction of the flow are viewed by a man as something unpleasant only because these changes do not coincide with his plan.

The concealed piece of truth in the above mentioned saying weighs much more heavily. The thing is that if you decide that from now on you will perceive any apparent unpleasant change to your scenario as positive, then it will definitely be that way. Such a statement could seem both harmless, and dubious. But we shall talk about that in the next chapter.

Moving along the flow of variations, you could speed up your progress with the help of "an oar" – visualizing a link of the transfer chain. In contrast to a slide, the visualization process includes the scenario of your movement towards the goal. But, as you know, visualizing the current link doesn't include the entire scenario, but only a small piece of what that is relevant to the present moment. You are moving your feet, while being guided by current intention. When making a step, you intend at the same time to make the next one.

Recall, how a mother watches her child grow. Every moment she keeps visualizing the current link of the transfer chain. This chain is divided into the smallest of links. The mother is happy that today her child got up onto his little legs, and she is imagining how tomorrow he will probably make his first step. The mother is not trying to imagine her child grow up and become an adult right before her eyes. She takes joy in the present and cherishes the current moment, convinced that tomorrow another success is waiting.

You should practice visualizing the current stage on your way to your goal according to the same principle as above. *Today is better than yesterday, and tomorrow will be even better than today.* There is no point anticipating all upcoming turns in the flow of variations. It is better to get pleasure out of the current moment and to simply keep moving your feet dispassionately and irreproachably. Let's say you want to take a swim in a pool. To do that, you would need to run a hundred meters, jump in and start swimming. And now imagine how you "dive" into earth and start moving your arms, not having reached the pool. Silly, isn't it? It is just as silly trying to visualize the subsequent links of the chain and to think about the means of achieving the goal.

While visualizing the current link, you are verifying that in the current moment things are going well. Everything is good. On that basis you build another step: tomorrow it will be even better. In your mind you intend to move on to the next step that is above the current step. Thus, a feedback chain is created. As a result, moving towards your goal could be viewed as moving up the stairs. The approaching success is not imagined as a cloud, hanging in the air, but rather as stairs, where each step supports the subsequent one. The level of success is gradually increasing, just like getting up the stairs. Every day carries in it a little piece of your future success. *Do not worry about the future, live through the present.*

On your way to your goal, pendulums will try in different ways to get you off track. Take any failure as a matter of course. Nothing could be going a hundred percent smoothly. When you are getting upset because of some failure of yours, the current step breaks, and you roll down the stairs. It makes you angry and dissatisfied with yourself, because the plan of your mind was ruined. Thus, you swallowed the bait of pendulums. If you are dissatisfied with yourself, then you will never move over to the life tracks where happiness and success is waiting for you. After all, are you happy with yourself when you are successful and well-off? How should you then get to these tracks, if the parameters of your personal radiation are tuned into you being dissatisfied with yourself?

Keep in mind that your mind perceives an unforeseen change in the flow of variations as a failure only because it is not part of his scenario. Why wouldn't you be able to perceive this change as a matter of course and to view this failure as success? Play the following game: *meet any supposed failure with joyous surprise instead of disappointment.* After all, it is external intention at work, and it moves you towards your goal in a, to you, mysterious way. And how could your mind know what particular path will lead you to your goal? The mind believes that the goal is hard to achieve just because he doesn't see that one path that leads to your goal among the beaten tracks. Of course, you won't achieve anything, if you won't submit to the flow of variations and if you won't get onto the path, onto which external intention is pushing you.

You shouldn't be looking at how others are going towards success, and trying not to fall behind. Do not fall for the herd instinct; you have your own destiny. The majority of people are walking along the beaten track, but only a few achieve true success – those, who didn't follow the rule "do as I do" and went their own way.

And so, a final warning. If you associate your dream with helping your loved ones, then there is a risk that it won't work out. For example, if you are thinking that once your dream comes true, then I'll be able to help them. The soul is egoistic in her nature. She is already getting only the smallest part of what she wants out of life. And to think about someone else's happiness on top of that, doesn't seem possible at all to her. The soul doesn't care about others, no matter how loved or precious they are to you. The soul cares only about her well-being. Her life in this world – is a rare and unique chance. Any altruistic manifestations, despite the popular opinion, come from the mind, and not from the soul. The soul will do everything possible to reach her goal. But if this goal doesn't serve her, but someone else instead, then the soul loses any interest and allows the mind the freedom to wear himself out in the struggle to solve one single task.

In the famous fairytale, the wooden boy Buratino[6] set his goal to get rich so that he could help his father. This is how he reasoned: I'll plant the golden coins in the field of Fortune, a golden tree will appear, and then I'll buy a theatre for Papa Carlo. Of course, the goal is not realized, but instead brings the wooden boy a lot of trouble. When setting the goal, Buratino made two big mistakes.

First mistake: the goal does not serve himself, but other people. The soul of Buratino is dreaming about what she wants, while the mind is thinking about what's best for Papa Carlo. Altruism is a very nice quality, but if you have decided to dedicate yourself to serving others, then you will never be happy yourself. Seeing your happiness in serving something or someone, in helping the weak and the defenseless, to give up yourself for someone else's pursuit or idea – is nothing more than an illusion and self-deception. It is that situation when the mind is seriously trapped by a pendulum and sees his happiness only in serving that pendulum. No matter how much your mind is trying to convince himself that he found his happiness in serving other people or some high idea, the soul of such a person is deeply unhappy. She has been driven into a box, where she doesn't even have any powers left to claim her right to happiness. The conviction of the mind that someone else's idea – is his, and that someone else's happiness – is his happiness, is a delusion of a person that haven't found his goal, or who, perhaps, haven't even looked for it.

Buratino's second mistake was that he considered money to be the means of obtaining the desired. As you remember, money cannot be a goal, or a means. It can only be a supplementary attribute on the way to the goal. There is no point in focusing your attention on the money. On the contrary, any thoughts about money usually only create more excessive potentials. If the chosen goal is yours, the money will come on its own. You won't need to worry about it at all. The fairy tale about Buratino is an excellent example of that.

It is being confirmed in the fairy tale that if you find your happiness yourself, then you will be able to bring joy to others. Because if you reach your goal, you will have money, well-being, and, of course, you will help your loved ones, because you will have the means to do that. But now, while you are still on your way to your goal, you should only be thinking about your happiness. By doing so you won't scare your soul away from the goal you have in mind. Allow your soul to only think about herself on her way to the goal. Once you have achieved the goal, you can allow your altruistic mind to help and care for your loved ones, nature, homeless animals, hungry children and whomever else.

Inspiration
You will be rushing on the crest of the wave, headed for your goal through the right door. The obtained comfort of your soul will allow you to transmit the radiation of harmony. In the chapter

about the wave of success, we have already talked about such a transmission. However, it is rather hard to intentionally summon a feeling of positive emotional arousal, and then to maintain it at all times. But now you get happy and calm because your soul and mind are in unity. Thus, the transmission will sort itself out. Everything will get better and a lot of problems will be eliminated on their own. You will often be visited by inspiration, unless you will try to summon it on purpose.

Inspiration is actually a great thing. It is only surrounded with a halo of mystery and incomprehensibility. It is believed that inspiration is something that is very hard to summon, it appears spontaneously and always when you least expect it. Inspiration is like a muse that accidentally just happened to drop by. Later, this muse could fly away just as suddenly as she appeared and not come back for a long time. The poor man is tediously waiting for the next time this lady will visit him, but he doesn't manage to attract her. Besides, it is not obvious at all whether it can be done.

In reality, everything is much easier than it seems. *Inspiration – is a state when your soul and mind are united, and there is no potential of importance.* The first part of this definition should be clear to you. Inspiration – is when you feel your soul rising, when there is a simple, easy and, above all, excellent flow to your creative process. It is absolutely clear that something like that could only take place when your soul and mind are in harmony. You will never experience inspiration, doing work that is not to your soul's liking.

By realizing your goal, you will, definitely, achieve the unity of your soul and mind, which is the first vital condition of inspiration. However, that condition is not enough. Why does inspiration suddenly appear, and then vanish? Perhaps it has to do with fatigue? But when you are inspired, you can work for many hours without feeling tired at all.

The second part of the definition will help you understand where inspiration comes from and where it goes away. You can probably already guess what I am talking about. The thing is that it is not that inspiration appears; rather it is simply being released when the potential of importance drops. What constitutes this importance? Firstly, fervent desire to reach the goal, and secondly, a persistent strive to get inspired.

By wanting to reach your goal, you won't reach it. I have already talked about it quite a few times. The longing desire to achieve a goal will, instead of giving rise to the wind of external intention, stir up the whirlwind of balancing forces that will quickly scare all your good fairies and muses away. The desire to summon inspiration is of the same nature. Any preparation and a subsequent wait for inspiration to come, creates an excess potential of importance.

You've thoroughly organized your working space, thought all the details through, put everything in order, had a good rest and made yourself ready. In other words, you have created the necessary setting for your meeting with the muse. By thoroughly preparing yourself you have already materialized the importance potential, and the wind of balancing forces starts howling outside your window. Now you've set the table, lit the candles and sat down, waiting for the unpredictable lady to come by. But she still won't come. And she will never come, you can be sure of that, because passive waiting – is desire squared. There is already a storm of balancing forces raging outside your window. Hence, no winged lady will ever get close to your house.

And if you will show impatience that is on the border with despair, then the raging wind will break your windows and turn the energy atmosphere of your house into chaos. The upheaval will grow a wall between your soul and your mind, so it will take you a long time to restore previous unity. You see what negative consequences your desire, preparation and waiting for inspiration will have?

Thus, inspiration won't appear until you release your death grip of waiting for inspiration to arrive. *Inspiration doesn't come to you - it is simply being released when the potential of importance goes away.* And the other way around, inspiration is bottled up when the impatient mind is driving the soul into the waiting box. The nasty habit of the mind to put everything under his volitional control ruins the entire celebration.

And still, despite the fact that inspiration seems impossible to control or predict, the mind has a specific way of establishing control over it. Yet, that control of his should have a different direction all together. As usual, the mind is beating against the closed window with his internal intention, while there is an open window just beside him. So, actually what you need to do – is to do the exact opposite.

Firstly, *abandon the desire to reach your goal.* Your goal won't go anywhere anyhow, if it is your goal that is. Sooner or later it will be achieved. The determination to have, without pushing and any decisiveness on your part, plays the most important role. You are calmly and without insisting taking what is yours, as you would be getting your mail from the mailbox. Internal intention should only be moving your feet, while you are walking up to that mailbox.

Secondly, *abandon any preparation for "the mystery".* Any preparation to get inspired, no matter what it entails, results in the creation of excessive potential. When you are preparing, it means that you want to attract something that you do not have. The more thorough your preparatory ritual, the worse will be your outcome. Do remember that you have already been in situations when you were preparing very diligently for something, an event or a meeting. It all failed in the end, the plan was spoiled or the meeting was cancelled. If the balancing forces are able to disrupt the interaction of material objects, then they will definitely not have any trouble blowing the barely tangible inspiration away, as if it was a tiny dust particle.

Thirdly, *abandon any waiting for the inspiration to come.* What's characteristic of inspiration is that it appears when you least expect it, right? Then why should you be waiting for it and thereby destroying the very condition for its appearance?

So, let's say you have fulfilled all three of these conditions. What is left of your inner intention? Only the determination to keep moving your feet – that is, to act. Simply start doing your thing. Without inspiration. That is when it will appear. *Inspiration will be released in the working process.* You won't be able to completely disseminate the potential of desire and waiting until you start acting, doesn't matter if it is done well or poorly. As you know, active intention disseminates any excess potential.

As a result, you get the following picture. You are setting the table for yourself, lighting the candles for yourself, making yourself comfortable and start drinking tea for your pleasure, not waiting around for anyone to appear. You can be sure that the fussy muse will be hurt by such indifference. How could you forget about her? She will instantly appear and make you company. That's all there is to it.

Reanimating the Goal

What to do, if you were walking towards someone else's goal, but do not want to abandon it? Can you achieve the goal of another person? Of course, you can. By arming yourself with the Transurfing technique you get a huge advantage in comparison to those, who do not know the rules in the world of pendulums. However, in order to achieve someone else's goal, you would need to make much greater effort, and you should be aware of that. You should follow the same principles in pursuing someone else's goal, as the ones you would use to pursue your own. The difference is only that all these principles will have to be followed to a hundred percent. That is about all I could say about achieving someone else's goal.

Let's assume that the goal you have chosen is actually someone else's. Would you like me to advise you: whether you should abandon it or not? If that is the case, then you have not yet completely grasped the principles of Transurfing. In this book, you are only given a map of the area and the rules of the game are revealed to you. But you are the one to make the decision. If you are not ready to take the responsibility for your fate, Transurfing won't help you. Its methods work only if you take the steering-wheel of intention into your hands. You now know how to handle this steering-wheel. But where you will be moving – is up to you. Only pendulums can provide you with readymade solutions. *By using someone else's solutions, you are giving your fate away into someone else's hands.*

If it is too late to abandon someone else's goal, then you could very well manage to achieve it. You would need to completely free yourself of desire and importance. There are plenty of obstacles on the way to someone else's goal, but the majority of these are created by the mind, when he is trying to fight the flow of variations and when he raises the level of importance. *Rent yourself out.* Act in a detached way, yet maintain awareness at the same time. Do not fight problems and obstacles. Drop importance, and the problems will disappear on their own.

Let's suppose that you were moving towards your goal, but you encountered several obstacles that are hard to overcome. What made them appear? Now you will be able to determine that quite easily. Make an analysis – where did you elevate the level of importance? What did you attribute an excessively important significance to? Where were you trying to fight the flow of variations? Drop importance, rent yourself out, rely on the flow of variations, and everything will be ok.

There is another reason to why your goal doesn't yield to you – perhaps you are walking towards it through someone else's door? Maybe you should take a look around and choose another door? But before changing your door, you absolutely have to drop importance and then see what happens. *Even your door could shut before you, if you have greatly elevated the level of importance in something.* For example, you would have greatly elevated the level of importance if you have put everything at stake. In that case, achieving that goal will be of enormously great significance to you. The door will be reopened, if you drop importance and secure a safety net, a back-up.

Usually, the door of another person that previously seemed so available and open, all of a sudden shuts before you. There will be a rather reasonable excuse, so your mind will only have to take off his hat and be at a loss: "Who could have known?" This situation is the opposite of that when the mind is thinking about the means of realizing the goal and does not see any real ways or doors to achieve the goal. But the point is that if the goal is true and you are ready to let yourself have, then your doors are opened just as suddenly, as those of others are closed. If you allow yourself to have, even the doors of others will be opened before you.

In any case, both your goal and your door are not one of a kind, there could be several. Thus, *it is never too late to look for a new goal, even if some of your former goals are objectively already unattainable.* You could try to attain someone else's goal, to walk through someone else's door and at the same time look for your own goal and door. You do not have to immediately drop what you have started. The transfer to the track of your goal could be done smoothly. You could work for someone else's goal and at the same time play the slide of your goal in your mind. Then, external intention will gradually open the invisible doors to you, which will allow you to painlessly change what you are doing.

It is unlikely that you will manage to free yourself completely from those pendulums that try to impose the doors of others onto you. It is most likely that you were previously forcing your way through these doors. But even now, when you possess certain knowledge, you are not safe from making mistakes. Everyone is bound to make mistakes. Just don't despair or blame yourself for your mistakes. You will find your door in the end. He, who doesn't make mistakes, doesn't try. You are surrounded by a whole lot of people that are "simply" living their life. They do not set any goals for themselves and they do not read books like this one. They want more than they have, but they do not have the intention to act. The advantage of people like that is that they do not make mistakes. But you will most definitely make mistakes, so just let yourself make them. *True success will grow on the ruins of your failures.*

When you are forcing your way through someone else's door, you will unavoidably encounter difficulties. From the outside, everybody will see that you are overcoming difficulties and are fighting problems. That's on the outside. Yet, no one, not even you, will see that you soul is resisting the compulsion to walk through someone else's door in any way possible. Your mind is pressing with his will, saying that you have to fight until the end. But even the soul of the most will-powered people is unable to bear this pressure. There is risk of a break-down. The annoying thing is that the break-down will appear in the shape of an unforgivable blunder. When a person experiences a break-down like that, he is making basic mistakes. Everyone is prone to making mistakes, even "the high and mighty".

On the way through someone else's door, break-downs will be waiting for you, and you will make mistakes. Just do not allow for any blunders. *Renting yourself out, act impeccably.* The paradox is that a big mistake could be forgiven. No one will forgive a small blunder. Do not look for sympathy, not even from your loved ones. And if these loved ones are even a little bit dependent on you, financially or socially, then you should definitely not look for any support from them – after all, you didn't justify their hopes.

Accusers and manipulators do not set any high goals before themselves, and that is why they do not make mistakes. Do not give them any reason to accuse you of unforgivable small blunders. *Act impeccably when it comes to small things.* Then a break-down on your way through someone else's door won't be as painful.

You should be especially cautious of the advice your loved ones are giving you. After all, they "wish you the best with all their heart". (Sometimes it is terrifying watching tender-hearted parents determining the final goal for their young child beforehand.) If you are persistently walking down your path, and then suffer a defeat, do not expect any mercy from your loved ones. They'll start yelling: "Didn't we tell you so! But you never listen!" You are extremely vulnerable in a moment like that. You are very upset by your failure, while the manipulators surrounding you take advantage of your vulnerability and try to get their hands on you. It is better for them this way. This is how they strengthen themselves, and plus you are already here, close at hand - all resigned and humble.

A person that finds himself in a tight corner is always surrounded by advisors and manipulators. All of them are only pursuing their own goals: either to grow in their own eyes, by teaching the loser, or to get an opportunity to manipulate you, or to simply put you in your place. Their favorite words, wrapped with "their sincere concern", when translated, go something like this: "Where are you going? What, are you supposed to be better than us? Sit down here with us and keep your head down. Live like us. We know life better." In the moment of weakness doubt will creep in: "Perhaps they are right, and I do not understand anything?"

The question arises as to whether you should listen to advisers and manipulators? What is it they are right about? They are only right about the fact that you made a mistake. Trying to achieve something, everyone will in any case make mistakes, even if one were to follow the advice of "smart people". But only you can find your goal. *No one else* can do it. Even those, who sincerely wish you only the best, cannot look into your soul. After all, even you hear your soul as the rustling of the morning stars, meaning that you practically cannot hear it. *Do not submit to someone else's influence. Believe in yourself.* In your search for your goal, do not listen to anyone or anything but your heart. When it comes to this matter, you must be firm and uncompromising towards the pendulums and you must pay close attention to your soul.

As you see, the only reservation in the process of choosing one's fate is the fact that not all goals and doors in the space of variations are yours. It doesn't at all mean that you cannot choose them. No one forbids you to do that, but if you do choose someone else's door - expect trouble. And do you really need it? By choosing the goals and doors of others, you are walking along the path of maximum resistance. The whole beauty of the freedom of choice is that personal goals and doors are much better for everyone than any goals and doors of other people. But in order to obtain the freedom of choice, you must free yourself from the influence of pendulums that impose the goals and doors of others onto you.

Summary

Someone else's goal – is always a case of an obligation, of forcing and making yourself do something you do not want to do.
Someone else's goal appears under the guise of fashion and prestige.
Someone else's goal tempts you with being so unachievable.

Someone else's goal makes you prove something to yourself and everyone else.

Someone else's goal is imposed on you by others.

Someone else's goal serves to improve the well-being of others.

Someone else's goal gives rise to the feeling of discomfort in your soul.

The achievement of your goal will cause the fulfillment of the rest of your desires.

What is your soul into? What will make your life a joyous and happy one?

Do not think about the means of achieving your goal until you have identified your goal.

Having made a decision, become aware of your soul's emotional comfort. The constraint of your soul could be eliminated by using slides. Her discomfort, however, can never be eliminated.

You soul always knows exactly what she doesn't want.

The objective of your mind in the process of looking for your goal is not to look for a goal.

The objective of your mind is to let all external information pass through him, paying particular attention to the state of emotional comfort of your soul.

Your door is the path that will lead you to your goal.

If the path is unknown, keep playing the slide of your goal in your mind. External intention will open your door to you on the life track of your goal.

If you are inspired on the way to your goal, then it is your door.

Everything that you can do naturally and with pleasure has significance and value.

Do not include any scenarios into the slide of your goal. You already have all of that.

Do not make your goal and door the only option. Find a safety net.

Do not shut your former door and do not burn your bridges.

Do not submit to the influence of others. Believe in yourself.

ENDNOTES

1. Meaning: you might consider something to be very difficult or frightening, but you are still doing it. Example: a student is worried about the immense amount of reading he has to do, but he does it anyway.

2. Matt 9:29

3. *The Tinder-box* (1835) is the first published work by the Danish writer Andersen, H.C., who is perhaps most known for his fairy tale *The Little Mermaid* (1836).

4. Théophile Gautier – a 19th century French poet, dramatist, novelist, journalist, and literary critic. (tran.)

5. Zeland, V. *The Model of Variations,* Chapter II - Pendulums

6. *The Adventures of Buratino* - a Russian fairy tale by Tolstoy, A. Buratino sets out to help his overworked father and liberate his friends – the puppets - from the tyrannical rule of the puppet master. In the end of the story, after a long struggle against the evil puppet master and his villains; Buratino, his friends – the puppets and Papa Carlo find a secret way to a new, magic theatre, which they then run themselves. (tran.)

BOOKS

mySpiritRadio